Social Deviance

POLITY SHORT INTRODUCTIONS

Nicholas Abercrombie, *Sociology*
Michael Bury, *Health and Illness*
Raewyn Connell, *Gender, Second Edition*
Hartley Dean, *Social Policy*
Lena Dominelli, *Introducing Social Work*
Jeffrey Haynes, *Development Studies*
Stuart Henry, *Social Deviance*
Stephanie Lawson, *International Relations*
Chris Rojek, *Cultural Studies*

Social Deviance

Stuart Henry

polity

The right of Stuart Henry to be identified as Author of this Work has been asserted in accordance with the UK Copyright, Designs and Patents Act 1988.

First published in 2009 by Polity Press

Polity Press
65 Bridge Street
Cambridge CB2 1UR, UK

Polity Press
350 Main Street
Malden, MA 02148, USA

ISBN-13: 978-0-7456-4303-8
ISBN-13: 978-0-7456-4304-5(paperback)

A catalogue record for this book is available from the British Library.

Typeset in 10 on 12 pt Sabon
by SNP Best-set Typesetter Ltd., Hong Kong
Printed and bound in Great Britain by MPG Books Limited, Bodmin, Cornwall

The publisher has used its best endeavours to ensure that the URLs for external websites referred to in this book are correct and active at the time of going to press. However, the publisher has no responsibility for the websites and can make no guarantee that a site will remain live or that the content is or will remain appropriate.

Selected quotes have been reproduced with permission of the publisher from: Stuart Henry and Roger Eaton, eds. 1999. *Degrees of Deviance: Student Accounts of Their Deviant Behavior*. Salem, WI: Sheffield Publishing Company.

Every effort has been made to trace all copyright holders, but if any have been inadvertently overlooked the publishers will be pleased to include any necessary credits in any subsequent reprint or edition.

For further information on Polity, visit our website: www.politybooks.com.

Contents

Preface   vii

1   What is deviance?   1

2   Why people ban behavior   25

3   Why some people break rules: from extreme to
    mundane deviance   44

4   Neutralizing morality and deviant motivations   57

5   How people become deviants   75

6   Responding to deviant designations and
    coping with stigma   93

7   Becoming normal: the politics of stigma   109

Conclusion: what can studying social deviance do for you?   122

References   129
Index   137

Preface

This short book explores the meaning of social deviance in contemporary society. It shows students of sociology how human actors create deviance by stereotyping others' different behavior, appearance, or ideas and judging them negatively. It explains what kinds of behaviors are banned as offensive or unacceptable, and who bans them. It exposes the important political process behind the creation of rules that lead to some people's behavior being sanctioned and others' behavior being celebrated.

Following the selective banning of behavior is a cycle of labeling and deviancy amplification that can send deviant actors into subterranean secret worlds that provide excuses, justifications, and rationalizations for their acts, which support continued, even expanded, social deviance. Ultimately *Social Deviance* explains the underlying process of how some people get sucked into deviant lifestyles from which there appears to be no escape, while others seek out these alternative domains. The book highlights the central role of social stigma on a person's moral identity. At its core *Social Deviance* looks at who becomes deviant and why. It delves into the multiple motives that cause rule-breakers to behave badly, at least in the eyes of those they offend, and it reveals the ways deviants think about their actions, their moral identity, and their fellow moral outcasts.

This book draws on several influences, not least the inspiration of the late Steven Box, my professor of sociology at the University of Kent, on whose interactionist insights in *Deviance, Reality and Society* I was nurtured. Steve Box was my mentor and window into the academic world of deviance. He taught me that my own working-class South London life vibrated with deviant insights, and that these were not only barriers that had nearly stopped me from going to university, but also nuggets of social life through which I could earn a doctorate in deviant behavior! What an astounding revelation to a 20-year-old from a council flat (in the United States, this is equivalent to "the projects"), who hadn't even believed it possible to get a bachelor's degree, and who had so disappointed his father for abandoning that £5-a-week apprenticeship (equivalent to £30 a week in 2007) with Decca for "book learning," which, he asserted, "won't earn you a living."

Steve was not easy to know but you couldn't be around him without being charged with questions about why things were the way they seemed and what was going on in the underbelly of society. In spite of his academic success, this fellow working-class Londoner – like his buddy in the heady 1970s, University of Kent deviance instructor Jock Young – never lost sight of his working-class roots. But where we start isn't where we have to end. As a working-class South London friend once commented: "Back when I knew you Stuart, you didn't have two words to rub together!" Where I come from, that would be a compliment.

My own studies in deviance resonated so well with those of former Arizona State University sociologist Erdwin "Bud" Pfuhl that he invited me to co-author the third edition of his social constructionist textbook *The Deviance Process* (Pfuhl and Henry, 1993). Many of the ideas in this book are a direct result of our collaboration. I would also be remiss if I did not acknowledge the contribution of external reviewers Erich Goode and Peter Adler to this book. It was Erich who recommended that I write this book, and he who made a significant impact on its quality by providing extensive and detailed feedback on a first draft that enabled the current revised version to be relatively smooth, streamlined and informative. It is to our great benefit that Erich's contributions to the field have been so extensive that they continue to be felt in significant and facilitating ways.

Finally, and significantly, students in my deviance behavior classes over the years have influenced this book, not only affecting my thinking about the issues of social deviance, but also in holding my feet to the ground in spite of my elevation into the ivory tower. Many of their thoughts about their own deviance were contained in *Degrees of Deviance* (Henry and Eaton, 1999); indeed, my co-editor, Roger Eaton, was one such student. In *Social Deviance*, I draw heavily on the words and ideas from these students, colleagues and faculty who have been significantly quoted to illustrate key concepts, and to capture the feel of the field.

The objective of this book, then, is not to provide a complete coverage of the field of social deviance, for that will come in classes and textbooks, writing and research as you explore this fascinating world. What I intend through this short introduction is to spark your deviance imagination. No more, no less.

1

What is deviance?

To study deviance is to study uncertainty. Students of deviance are looking at society's edge. Whose edge or what edge, and why it even is an edge, are all uncertainties to be discovered by students of deviance. But we encounter certainties as well, one of them being the wide range of behaviors, demeanors, identities, appearances, styles, attitudes, and beliefs regarded as deviance. This is because what's deviant varies from one individual, society, culture, social context, and historical era to another. Views differ on how deviant actors and judgmental audiences interact and interrelate.

At its simplest, the sociology of deviance is the systematic study of social norm violation that is subject to social sanction. But "behind this seemingly simple and clear-cut definition, however, lurks a swarming host of controversies" (Adler and Adler, 2006: 3) not least because the study of deviance is also the study of the politics of social life on the edge. In this political conflict we find two clearly identifiable positions, one known variously as the "relativist" or "social constructionist" position and the other known as the "absolutist" or "realist" position: "Each perspective has its own mission, agenda, enterprise, and methodology" (Goode, 2007: 1075). From the relativist/constructivist perspective, deviance is "lodged in the eye of the beholder rather than in the act itself, and it may vary in the way it is defined by time and place." This perspective "sees deviance as 'subjectively problematic,' ... and takes as its primary task an understanding of how judgments of deviance are put together and with what consequences." At the opposite extreme, the absolutist perspective sees deviance as possessing predetermined or universal features such that "something obvious within an act, belief, or condition makes it different from the norm in everybody's eyes," and that at "its fundamental core it embodies the unambiguous, objective 'essence' of true or real deviance." Explanatory theories from this perspective "regard deviance as 'objectively given,' that is, a syndrome-like entity with more or less clear-cut, identifiable properties whose causal etiology can be explicated by the social scientist" (Goode, 2007: 1075–6). As we will see, the sociological definition of deviance embodies aspects of both these positions.

In this book you will learn about the social processes and the political practices of the actors and audiences that constitute the deviance enterprise. On the way you'll discover the excitement, fun, creativity, and chaos, as well as the pain, shame, and suffering, that accompanies the world of deviance as it straddles the edge of socially defined normality. I hope that you will also develop an appreciation, if not always sympathy, for the "deviant imagination."

Normality, difference, and deviance

As sociologists have long pointed out, something is deviant only in relation to what is normal. But what is normal, what is conventional, and who gets to decide? Normality implies a common set of shared cultural values and rules or norms about how to behave, appear, or think. Behaving differently, looking differently, thinking differently, in violation of those norms and values, can all be considered social deviance. Social deviance includes everything from minor norm- or rule-violating behavior to behavior that breaks criminal or other laws designed to ban or prohibit it. People may classify, as social deviants, those who participate in different behavior from their own, and those classified may or may not accept their designated deviant identity. Whether they are so classified, and whether they accept or reject the deviant label, are the outcomes of the social processes that create deviance. These processes involve the interpretation of the meaning of their act, and meaning is critically affected by historical and social context. In 1970 a person walking alone down the street apparently talking to themselves might be considered to be schizophrenic, or at the very least mentally disordered; in 2008 the same action on the same street would be interpreted as someone talking on their cell phone via a Blue Tooth device.

As well as differences in behavior, deviance can also include having and/or displaying certain physical attributes that others consider deviant, such as stuttering, or being excessively short, physically disfigured, fat, or thin. Bulimics and anorexics, for example, can be considered deviant, but they might also be considered "sick," as suffering from a mental disorder, and as a result of such an interpretation of the meaning of their appearance, the way they are seen and treated varies. Indeed, while the mentally disordered, in general, are often considered deviant, that is often because of their bizarre and sometimes threatening behavior, rather than having an odd appearance.

Thinking abnormal thoughts, whether or not these are reflected in behavior, can also be considered deviance. Historically, deviant thought was equated with sinful thought, even heretical thought, and has resulted in extreme forms of punishment, from being excommunicated and tortured to being executed, and sometimes by being burned alive. Even today, in many parts of the world, political differences of thought can result in imprisonment without trial (e.g. under Mugabe's rule in Zimbabwe) because of the threat they pose to the powerful. Although in a postmodern world "thinking outside the box" implies that deviance can also be positive, this is not the case if that thinking is so far outside the box that those in it feel threatened.

So, a key quality of deviance is *difference*, and a critical component of social deviance is how that difference relates to what is seen as normal, expressed through a common set of values and norms. But there is more to social deviance than mere difference. In the USA and Europe someone with naturally red hair is different, but not seen as socially deviant because of it (although British comedy actress Catherine Tate has shown in her "Gingers for Justice" skit that deviance, sanction and stigma can be inferred by those with red hair!). Difference from what is seen as normal, therefore, does not necessarily mean that someone is socially deviant. In contrast, someone with dyed blue or spiked hair is statistically different but also may be seen as socially deviant, especially if they also wear tattoos and display ring piercings. Difference of thought or viewpoint, or clothing or cuisine, is respected as a right and is "seen to contribute to the vitality and creativity of modern society." In contrast, deviance is "a culturally unacceptable level of difference" that is subject to suspicion, surveillance, regulation, sanction, or penalty by society's social control agencies, because it is seen as posing a "threat to the social fabric" (Sumner, 2006: 126).

Erich Goode has pointed out that it is worth reflecting on the relationship between difference and deviance. First, some forms of "deviance" are based on imputed, putative, or imaginary difference – such as the designation and persecution of witches in Renaissance Europe or in New England's infamous Salem witchcraft trials of 1692. There was no "difference" as such. There was a sociological difference in that people who were designated as witches tended to be female, older (though not in Salem), more socially marginal, etc. – but no difference with respect to the putative deviance. Second, even where an audience interprets "difference," a critical question is how much "difference" is interpreted as difference? There are vast stretches of behavior, appearance, or ideas within a continuum of difference that aren't noticed, then suddenly, at a certain point along the continuum, a "difference" is noticed. So even "difference" is socially constructed. As Erich poignantly asks: When does a "difference" *make* a difference?

Sociologists define deviance as an identified difference that the members of a society regard as morally offensive or threatening. For social deviance to occur, therefore, we need both a judging audience and a deviant actor. Each has a "social" basis. The sociological perspective that recognizes the social basis of deviance in the audience is called "social constructionism."

Social constructionism: audiences create deviance?

In order for behavior, appearance, or beliefs to be seen as deviant, they have to be "constructed" as such by a social audience around identified differences. Constructing deviance requires a negative judgment to be made about departures from norms. To make such a negative judgment, and for a behavior to be designated as social deviance, the audience, comprising someone or some group, has to make a series of decisions. The audience decides: first, what the shared values are; second, to whom they apply; third, whether any particular case of behavior, appearance, or thought is a violation of these cultural norms and values; and fourth, whether the violation is of sufficient seriousness or significantly offensive to do something about. Social constructionism then is a process that defines what (behavior, appearance, beliefs) are regarded as deviant. What is decided can vary depending on the society so that different societies have different definitions of deviance. What is defined as "deviance" can also vary according to one historical time period versus another, one context versus another, and, within the same society, from one social circle or community to another. Social constructionism then determines what, where, and, historically, when behavior, appearance, or beliefs are designated as deviance. Particular audiences determine all of these variations in the social construction of deviance: the audience varies, hence the social construction of the behavior may also vary, or the audience may make similar judgments resulting in similar constructions of deviance. This is because audiences are collective entities that vary from small groups to whole societies, each of which has its own values and norms common to its members, but also shares common norms or values across the groups and also across societies. This means that there can be both differences in the way deviance is constructed and commonalities. So let's look at who these different audiences are and at some examples of the variations in what counts as deviance to them.

Who exactly are the audience? Is it humanity in general? Is it the culture of a society, or do we begin at the level of communities within a society? Should we instead stay within subcultures of a society, or only consider deviance at the level of groups and, if so, would deviance then be in relation to the group or are we talking about the deviance of the group from society or from other groups? Erich Goode makes the point that judgments of deviance are always in relation to some group's judgment – an act is deviant "to" a particular audience and it doesn't have to be a society as a whole. Abortion is deviant *to* the majority of Right-to-life Catholics; using a position of power to obtain sexual pleasure is deviant to feminists; and, of course, some judgments are more widespread than others. Consider, first, the variation in defining deviance from one society to another, based on their different *cultures*. In nearly all US cities, women going topless would be seen as deviant behavior but women going topless on the French Riviera, in Rio, or within tribal societies in Africa is considered normal. But even within different cultures, one behavior might be considered acceptable or deviant by the members of the society, depending upon the social structure. For example, adultery is both commonplace, expected, and, yet, deviant to the members of the Kaliai Lusi-speaking tribe of Papua New Guinea. Indeed, for this small-scale horticultural community, whether an act of adultery is deviant depends not so much on whether it breaks rules, as on whether, in doing so, it also causes conflict and the disruption of social relationships. A promiscuous woman who hops from man to man is labeled as a "frog," but rather than this being a derogatory term it is a gossip framing that forms the basis for discussions about the details of affairs, which is accompanied by as much humor and joking as mild condemnation. In contrast, a man who seduces his brother's wife may create an intra-lineage conflict among members of the kinship group. The conflict that results arises because the adulterous or illicit affair violates a man's rights in the sexuality of a woman over whom he has control. This kind of adultery would be considered inhuman, animal-like behavior. It is serious because the society is structured (organized) around systems of descent such that

> sexual intercourse with the woman who is responsible for social repro-
> duction of the group is the ultimate sin and must be treated with the
> utmost severity . . . it is a violation of the moral order. It is not human
> behavior: people who do it are said to be "people who act like
> dogs" . . . people are reluctant to talk about such behavior . . . They do

not joke or tease about it. It is never a subject of casual gossip. The mere suggestion that others suspect a person is engaging in a sexual relationship with an affine may result in suicide. (Counts and Counts, 1991)

Now consider social *context*. Two people make love in a hotel; making love in the lobby of a hotel is considered deviant whereas making love in a hotel room is not – although if the people making love are cheating on other relationships, this may constitute deviance from a person's *social role*. Wearing a bikini on a beach is acceptable because beaches are one of the socially defined appropriate contexts for wearing bikinis; wearing a bikini in a house of worship is not appropriate. Finally, within the same society, there is variation among social circles – one "group" to another, one category in the population, and one community to another. Gay relationships in San Francisco, the Hillcrest area of San Diego, or the Chelsea area of New York are expected; and acceptable gay relations in Salt Lake City or Chelsea, Michigan, are not, or are at least much less expected or accepted. By its very nature, the construction-ism through which people define and interpret actions or appearances is always "social." The social construction of deviance by audiences can be particularly evident when cultures collide or come together as they do in an increasingly globalized world.

The idea of social deviance as the result of cultural conflict arose in the late 1930s in the United States. Put simply, learning the norms to conform to one culture can result in deviance in another culture. This was especially a problem in the era of mass immigration to the United States in the 1920s and 1930s, but it is also a problem in an increasingly globalized world where we come into contact with people from many other cultures and subcultures. While globalization unifies societies around certain cultural consumer themes and institutions, from McDonald's to Microsoft and from blue jeans to Coke, it also throws into contrast cultural differences that, to some, appear deviant. For example, some Muslim girls wear make-up, and blue jeans under their burkas, which may seem as incongruous as Nike producing a line of sportswear for Muslim women that preserves their modesty, since the Koran requires women to cover everything except their faces, hands, and feet. Issues of social deviance also arise when Muslims living in the West confront this culture conflict in their own homes and follow the norms of their own culture to deal with the perceived threat. On December 10, 2007, in Canada, a Pakistani father, Muhammad Parvez, killed his 16-year-old daughter, Aqsa, for refusing to wear the hijab. Canadian police charged him with murder. Was this killing deviance or confor-mity? And by whose standards, and who gets to decide? In the Muslim community a child who does not wear the hijab, and, therefore, is deviant by traditional Muslim standards, brings shame to their family, who are considered failures by their community. In Pakistan, "honor killings" are a daily occurrence. Cultural conflict places those from one cultural tradition in conflict with those in another, putting them in a double deviancy situation. For example, as they struggle to reconcile Muslim and secular Western behavior and appearance, teenage Muslim girls are confronted with competing demands to fit in to the norms of different cultural audiences, represented, on the one hand, by their parents and, on the other, by their peers. As sociologist Jasmin Zine says, Canadian Muslim girls trying to deal with avoiding deviancy designations from conflicting cultures can become cultural chameleons:

Dressing in one manner at home and another at school is one way young Muslim girls in Canada are negotiating competing cultural demands . . . For some youth, what they do is develop a double persona. At home they're the good Muslim kid, they pray and they fast and go to mosque . . . When they go to school they become a different person. They create a persona to fit with the competing cultural demands of home and school . . . In addition to removing the hijab, some Muslim youth may also anglicize their name and wear makeup . . . When it is time to go home, they don the hijab. It is about fitting in. I don't think it's about shame. I don't think they dis-identify with being Muslim, they just remove the markers of that identity so that they are better able to fit in with the cultural code at school. Now the codes are very, very tough . . . the hijab is a way to identify oneself as Muslim . . . those who choose not to wear it . . . are then sometimes seen as being less pious, that they are leaving Islam . . . it's a very loaded [signal] from the perspective of the people viewing you. (Zine, quoted by Rook and Smithers, 2007)

Such cultural clashes over what counts as deviance can also occur between similar cultures with different norms in otherwise similar societies, such as those in the USA and Europe. Consider the case of the baby left crying in a stroller outside a barbecue restaurant in the lower East Village of New York while the parents were inside eating. Some concerned passer-by called the police and the parents were arrested for "endangering the welfare of a child." The parents were fully aware that their child was outside, were watching the child through the restaurant window and, even though the restaurant staff had tried to persuade them to bring the child into the restaurant, they refused: "The mother, a 30 year old actress from Copenhagen, said that in Denmark – where she was born – leaving children alone unattended in the street while their parents dine inside a restaurant, is the norm. She was utterly astonished at the rabble caused by her actions. . . . She claims it was a cultural faux pas, not a crime" (Boles, 1997). While New York may be a dangerous place, resulting in the actions of the parents being judged deviant and thereby subject to intervention and control by others, the fact that the Danish mother had a different cultural experience, in her view, justified her actions. She was simply following her Danish cultural norms rather than American – or even New York – ones!

As we've seen, the historical and social context also makes a difference as to whether a behavior will be judged deviant. In certain historical periods cigarette smoking has been considered medicinal, a status symbol, a normal adult behavior, a nasty irritating habit and, increasingly, a crime. Where it is done also makes a difference. Smoking in the isolation of one's home has been considered perfectly acceptable, provided other members of one's household have no objections to passive smoking effects. But smoking on school premises has always been frowned upon and is often considered grounds for expulsion, while smoking during the production and preparation of food for sale may be grounds for dismissal. Recently, smoking in some public places, including restaurants and bars and on airline flights, has been banned, and smoking violations have increasingly become subject to prosecution and fines. According to the website of the coalition SmokeFree Illinois, since January 1, 2008, all indoor workplaces and public places, including bars/taverns, restaurants, private clubs, and casinos, have been smoke-free. Smoking is prohibited around entrances and exits, windows that open and ventilation intakes. The aim of the law is to ensure "that all Illinois workers will have a workplace safe from secondhand smoke, and that all of us can breathe clean, smoke-free air when we eat out or spend a night on the town." People or establishments that violate the law are subject to fines ranging from $100–$250 (for individuals) to as much as $2,500 for businesses, whose fines also escalate for repeat offenses: "First Violation: Not less than $250; Second Violation: Not less than $500; Additional Violations: Not less than $2500" (SmokeFree Illinois, 2008).

Other examples of deviance might not involve specific behavior so much as group involvement, such as being a member of a Goth or vampire cult, being involved in a gang – such as the Crips or the Bloods – or an organization such as a nudist colony, or a vegetarian movement. Here the group's primary activities are counter to those seen as held in common by the wider society. And what about participating in groups whose aim is to counter what is considered a greater crime? Take, for example, animal rights activists. Gary Yourofsky, who travels the USA lecturing on animal rights and injustice as a member of Animals Deserve Adequate Protection Today and Tomorrow (ADAPTT) and as a representative of People for the Ethical Treatment of Animals (PETA), has been convicted and incarcerated for his activism and protests. In 1999 he was sentenced to six months in a Canadian maximum-security prison for a felony raid on a fur farm. He sees his activities as "civil disobedience" (of the kind exercised by Gandhi); his critics see him as a domestic terrorist. Indeed, he is featured on the website targetofopportunity.com dedicated to listing people this organization believes have "betrayed and endangered America by their Seditious, Treasonous, and/or Terrorist activities . . . operating under the false illusion of 'Peaceful' and 'Non-Violent' activism . . . [and who] present a serious threat to all Americans" (targetofopportunity.com, 2009). Clearly there is more involved in social deviance than the deviants themselves.

Not only can each society have groups of members whose behavior deviates from the cultural or contextual role expectation norms, so too can the behavior of members of these deviant groups be deviant from the norms of the group. Take the example of weight and human body size. In any particular society there is an average weight and size. Differences from the normal weight are wide ranging across a population, although for individuals weight ranges by only about 10 percent above or below what is considered a genetically determined set point. A subset of those with "obesity" is defined as "morbidly obese." The morbidly obese are perceived as deviant, with all kinds of assumptions made about the reasons for their appearance. Some of the obese form groups to combat their obesity and to lose weight. Members of these groups, such as Weight Watchers, must conform to an eating program designed to help them lose weight. Those who do not conform may feel shamed and, indeed, may be treated by other members of the group as deviant – now not only from the society as a whole but also from the norms of the WeightWatchers group. Similarly there are deviants among the members of self-help groups of alcoholics, such as Alcoholics Anonymous – themselves deviant from the population at large who are "social drinkers" – who see themselves as suffering from the "disease of alcoholism." These deviant AA members are not those who "slip" and lapse, as this is seen as part of the disease pattern. Rather, deviant AA members are those who display violations of the AA group protocol, and at meetings those who talk and act in ways contradictory to the expected behavior of an AA member, for which they are ridiculed and sanctioned by the group for their deviance. So, making deviance out of difference involves making meaning out of behavior, appearance, or thoughts in collaboration with others, and it involves a multi-stage process.

The process of social construction

To say that deviance is socially constructed – the relativist position – implies several things: (1) there is not one reality but as many realities as there are groups constructing the norms as their reality; (2) any appearance of a single dominating reality is largely an illusion in spite of claims about universal values; (3) there are many moralities reflecting multiple realities; (4) there are numerous stereotypes constructed by groups as part of their means to control and contain human behaviors that are seen to deviate from and threaten their view of what counts as reality; and (5) deviance does not just happen but is created by people making distinctions and acting towards those distinctions as though they are real.

Sociologists define a *moral panic* as an exaggerated, widespread concern that a particular group or segment of the population (deviants or "folk devils") is responsible for harm or a threat to the society. The fear of satanic ritual abuse cults that erupted in the United States and the United Kingdom in the 1980s offers a dramatic example of the moral panic concept. Moral panics may generate such heated concern and fear that the society enacts legislation designed to eradicate the threatening behavior, as was the case with satanic cults.

Acts may also be banned because of a desire to promote certain values and a particular set of values or lifestyle. Standards or norms can be precisely specified as rules or laws, or can be loosely constructed as informal norms and expectations. Laws, rules and norms are shaped by personal biographies, group pressures and processes, and by the wider societal context in which people live.

Sometimes behaviors or appearances, or ideas judged to be deviant, are the product of precisely the same process of social construction that is involved in constructing the standards of those who are judging their behavior unacceptable; one group's standards are another group's deviance. For example, when a government enacts food and drug legislation, making the unhygienic preparation of carcass meat unlawful, it is promoting a particular set of values and making deviants out of those who prepare meat in ways deemed to be unhygienic. When a group of vegetarians declares any meat preparation and consumption "killing," they are making deviants of, among other people, the US Food and Drug Administration. Both groups, however, are setting norms that are designed to promote a particular, albeit different, lifestyle. Deviance and convention are not isolated phenomena but exist in relation to each other and in relation to the wider societal and global structure in which they are set.

After differences in behavior have been identified and made significant, and after moralizing judgments have been drawn about their acceptability or unacceptability, another level of work by audiences and observers is evident in the process of constructing deviance. This involves equating the person engaging in social deviance with the negatively judged behavior. Here the whole person is reduced to a stigmatized status; a caricature extracted from part of their total behavior is taken to represent their most important features. Unlike much of modern society, the construction of stereotypes is not a product of the industrial revolution but of something inherently human.

The classification of a whole person on the basis of the kind of behavior that they engage in, or attributes that they display, is part of our shorthand way of dealing with the complexity and diversity of the world that we inhabit. While it might be more interesting, it would certainly be more time-consuming if we explored the total life of each person we met before judging them or classifying them. Instead we draw inferences from selected snippets of information and place them in a pre-existing category of our worldview. People whose behavior is odd or different or threatening create fear and anxiety, especially if their behavior is found to be disturbing or offensive according to some standard we value. So, instead of just classifying the behavior, we exaggerate the behavior as illustrative of that committed by a certain type of person, and that person is tagged or labeled as a deviant.

Importantly, however, the stereotypes designed to avoid or manage problematic or undesirable behavior are constructed in advance, in order to avoid future problems, and people are classified based on a variety of indicators, regardless of whether they fit the category or label. Consider the example of restaurant servers. In attempting to serve food and maximize their tips restaurant staff create categories of deviant customers through the use of stereotypes, based on whether they are likely to be good or bad tippers. These categories are used to classify customers, regardless of whether they have a particular history, or whether they are new to the restaurant. Normal customers, called "tippers," will give a "fair," though culturally determined, tip for service. In the USA good tippers will give 15–20 percent tips, or more. Bad tippers will give less than 15 percent, and are known as "stiffers." Stiffers are seen as deviant by restaurant staff because they do not know how to tip.

Designating a customer as a "tipper" or "stiffer" is based on a range of psychological scans and behavioral cues to do with dress, demeanor, speech, and eye contact, but also includes race, age, and gender. Restaurant staff believe that they need to master the technique of discriminating between customers if they are to increase their income from tips. "Tippers" are given good tables, booths, and good service. "Stiffers" are given a rough time, are given poorly located tables and are hurried through the restaurant to be replaced by "normal customers" who do know how to tip; of course, the effect is likely to be a self-fulfilling prophesy since this stereotype-based treatment will produce bad tips. Deviants, then, can be created as a by-product of trying to manage normal and routine behavior in the attempt to prevent problems from arising. This is known as the "theory of office" and we'll learn more about it in chapter 5.

Having seen the moral relativity of the ways different societies socially construct deviance, you might be wondering whether I am suggesting that there are no standards, and that everything is equal to everything else. You might ask me after that first lecture on "The Social Construction of Deviance,"

> But, Dr. Henry, just because societies and groups define and enact behavior differently, does this mean that the "realities" that other societies define and enact are right? Aren't the proponents of these alternate realities ignorant or mistaken? By accommodating to their differences aren't you helping to perpetuate the harm and pain that they cause others? Some people believe the Earth is flat, but they are wrong. Some societies believe in a monkey god, but they are also wrong. Was Jim Jones right to poison 909 of his followers, including children, in 1978, with cyanide laced *Flavor Aid* because he believed this "revolutionary suicide" was for the greater good of the People's Temple cult that he'd founded?

The answer I'd give is that, as a sociologist of deviance, my job is to help you to understand alternate moral universes as being equally valid to the non-Western ones, and to have you appreciate and be tolerant towards different behaviors that we consider deviant (e.g. "In Thai society, they eat bugs"). But if the society, or the community, or the subculture, group, or gang practices behavior that is more exploitative and repressive than ours ("In Saudi Arabia, physically beating a wife is acceptable provided she is not hit in the face and is only struck where the marks can't be seen"), then I am not saying that such behavior is an alternate definition of reality that is coequal with our own. If such behavior creates pain and suffering to others, then I am saying it is wrong.

However, this does not mean that all differences that we see as odd or deviant are wrong. The best I can do as a sociologist and teacher is to demonstrate the existence of alternate definitions of right and wrong and show that, within the context of alternate realities, this is how they work. I am not trying to convince you that alternate realities are equally as "true" and as valid as your own views. Clearly some moral "realities," and some alternate definitions and practices, are pretty difficult to defend:

infanticide, human sacrifice, marriage between eleven-year-old girls and fifty-year-old men, pedophilia, and, for that matter, the murder of a daughter for an act of social deviance. And there is some anthropological evidence that supports the case for such a more moderate social constructionist position.

Some anthropologists believe in "cultural universals." In other words, it is possible to identify several standard universal values across all cultures. No culture exists in which "in-group" members accept indiscriminate lying (so all value honesty), stealing (all value rights of property ownership), violence, and suffering (all value peaceful coexistence), or allow incest (all restrict sexual intercourse to non-familial adults). However, members of one cultural in-group did not necessarily hold those values for members of other cultures or "out-groups," and, as we've seen so far, what each culture defined as a value was culturally specific. So on the one hand, we have a roster of "primal crimes" that are punished in all societies; on the other hand, societies vary immensely in imposing other types of rules, highly variable from one society to another, that seem somewhat arbitrary, whose violation does not threaten the fabric of the society. This is an important distinction. Are rape, murder, and robbery social constructions in the same sense that, say, premarital intercourse is more strongly condemned in Iran than in Sweden, or that premarital intercourse was more condemned in the United States in the past than today? Yes, all forms of deviance are socially constructed in the sense that norms do not drop down from the sky, but some norms have always existed and don't vary substantially (that is, they exist everywhere and vary as to particulars), while others are recent and vary to the extent that they exist in some societies and don't in others.

The point is that, if we do not appreciate the social construction process, we are likely to regard all cultural differences as wrong, rather than just the extreme manifestations. In short, neither extreme relativism nor extreme absolutism is helpful here. What we need is a measured middle ground. Part of that comes from looking at the other half of the deviance equation, the deviant social actor.

Deviant motivations: actors create deviance?

It is clear from the analysis so far that audiences have a significant role in the creation of deviant behavior, and in the creation and production of deviant stereotypes. However, the second "social" basis of deviance addresses the mechanisms that influence or determine how someone comes to engage in behavior that is already defined as deviant. The sociologist of deviance must take into account whether some people are more likely to deviate than others, and whether some people are more likely than others to become deviant. We are concerned here with kinds-of-people theories. What leads a social actor to become socially deviant? There are several possible routes.

One route to deviance is participating in a group that encourages such behavior. If Aqsa, the Canadian Pakistani girl murdered by her father, had been brought up in a Pakistani community in her homeland, she would not have encountered the diverse ideas and values of the Canadian culture. She would not have experienced the Canadian teen peer-pressure that led her to stop wearing the hijab, seen as a seriously deviant act by her family's culture. So we can ask what led Aqsa to become a deviant actor by defying her family's traditional cultural values whereas others, recognizing the entrenched moral beliefs of Islam, and the likely reaction of parents and male siblings, do not do so.

When Gary Yourofsky took direct action to destroy a fur farm knowing that these actions were illegal, what led him to do so rather than engage in the non-violent political protest that he now practices, and that others practice? When alcoholics drink or crystal meth addicts use drugs – to the extent that it destroys their life, and perhaps the lives of their relatives, friends, or strangers – is that completely explained by the socially constructed ideas about the immorality of excessive drinking or the dangers of drug abuse? In the words of many alcoholics (especially those belonging to Alcoholics Anonymous), they have a disease called alcoholism. If so, then their excessive drinking and the behavior that follows from it would have followed anyway, even if some of the consequences, frequency, and duration might have been different if society's audiences had reacted differently.

And what about the morbidly obese? Do they have a choice about whether or not to eat to excess or to regulate their eating to match their body metabolism so that their appearance conforms to socially constructed stereotypes or the normal weight range? Sure, if there were not culturally produced, media-hyped, super-thin, waif-like images of women or slender muscular male role models, their obesity would perhaps be less of a social or public issue. But, if it is true for some that their condition is biologically or genetically produced – perhaps as a result of disease such as hypothyroidism and insulin production, or genetic defects affecting the leptin hormone brain chemistry, as argued by some psychiatrists, psychologists, geneticists, and nutritionists – then eating will make these people excessively fat. The condition of being morbidly obese, with or without a stigma attached, is a different condition from the majority of others in the population and likely to result in health, mobility, and employment issues (Comuzzie and Allison, 1998).

In other words, as well as being concerned with how deviance is socially constructed, sociologists of deviance explore how some people, rather than others, become deviant. Is it completely by chance or are some people more likely to become deviant actors? Related to this, we need to examine how someone enacts a particular form of deviance: how does one "become" a topless dancer, a juvenile delinquent, a serial murderer, a drug addict, an alcoholic, a political revolutionary, anorexic or bulimic, or a corporate fraudster?

Sociologists have identified a variety of routes to deviance, from individual biologically and psychologically rooted proclivities, including cognitive, developmental, and interactive social learning, to geographical, cultural, and structural forces (see chapter 3). For example, evolutionary socio-biologists argue that the genetic make-up of humans controls the pathways and trajectory of their life course. "Selfish genes" govern the pattern of our behavior. These genes strive to reproduce themselves through whatever means is necessary, including committing deviant acts, if doing so will improve their ability to procreate and expand the size of their gene pool. To the degree that a particular characteristic is prevalent in a population, including social deviance, "it is likely to have contributed to the reproductive success of the ancestors of the individuals currently living" (Ellis and Walsh, 1997: 232).

Some socio-biologists have, for example, developed a sensation-seeking/arousal theory of deviant behavior based on human brain chemistry. Under normal environmental conditions, as a result of a biological predisposition to low levels of dopamine and dopamine-like neurotransmitters called endorphins, some people have lower than normal emotional arousal. Whereas most people are excited by a wide range of stimuli found in their daily environment, dopamine-depressed people get bored easily. To increase their arousal to normal levels, or even to create accentuated levels of arousal, these people engage in super-challenging or intensely stimulating activities. Some of us surf in hurricanes, others street race, some hang-glide or engage in extreme sports, and yet others turn to deviance. Deviant behavior can provide this "on the edge" stimulation for "sensation seekers." Bio-social theorists argue that we can expect a higher level of deviance from sensation seekers than from those with normal sensitivities to stimulation, and they can also be expected to engage in higher levels of substance abuse that provides, albeit momentarily, elevated levels of excitation.

From this more absolutist perspective, human development through family, social, and organizational environments interacts with the human gene machine, and is adapted, even co-opted, to enhance the human organism's ability to dominate others. Socio-biologists argue that environmental contexts, together with each human organism's unique biology, shape their subsequent behavior patterns. Thus deviant behavior is seen to result from hereditary factors interacting with environmental ones. Together, these affect the brain and cognitive processes that in turn control behavior: "Behavior [deviant or otherwise] is not inherited; what is inherited is the way in which an individual responds to the environment. Inheritance provides an orientation, predisposition, or tendency to behave in a certain fashion" (Fishbein, 1998: 94).

While these kinds of individually rooted theories of deviance do not, in themselves, provide complete explanations for why some people, rather than others, become deviant social actors, together with the social constructionist explanations of why people ban behavior (chapter 2) they do help to explain the phenomenon. In later chapters, we will see that, even though some people's behavior is taken to be deviant – and regardless of whether it is biologically, psychologically or socially determined – they need not accept such socially constructed definitions of themselves and are often involved in the process of rejecting, deflecting, managing this stereotyping or labeling of their identity. They do so because it is their whole person, not just the behavior, that is now morally questionable.

Determining deviance

So how do we decide whether behavior is deviant or not? We might start with the familiar idea of statistical deviance. This idea is based on the fact that all behavior is distributed in a normal curve or "bell curve." Behavior that is commonly occurring forms the body of norms, whereas behavior on the extremes, which occurs less frequently, is designated as "deviant." Thus there can be both negative and positive deviance.

In one direction, the more extreme from the norm, the less frequent, and the more serious, is negative deviance; at the other end of the continuum is "positive deviance," such as being a genius, being academically gifted or exceptionally musically talented. Positive deviance applies to those who surpass conventional expectations in honorable ways.

The key factor in deciding what is deviance, from the statistical perspective, is how many people do it relative to the whole population. On this criterion, homosexuality is clearly negatively deviant from heterosexual relations. So too is bisexuality and transsexuality, but what about sexual affairs outside monogamous relationships or marital infidelity? Polls report that while 90 percent of Americans admit that adultery is wrong, 22 percent of men and 14 percent of women admit to having an affair outside their marriage; in Britain, a 2006 MORI survey revealed that 40 percent of the British population admit to being unfaithful.

Clearly social deviance can occur closer to the norm of the bell curve than its fringes!

However, sociologists generally hold that a departure from a statistical norm does not define deviance. Reading a book a day is statistically outside the norm, but it is not a type of deviance. Some sociologists, such as Erich Goode, believe that "positive deviance" – surpassing conventional expectations – is "a red herring." The key issue is what makes negative deviance have the qualities that it does?

An alternative approach to determining what "counts" as deviance is to consider whether the behavior violates a publicly stated law, rule, or moral code. French sociologist Emile Durkheim took the view that what counts as crime or deviance is behavior that "shocks the common consciousness" or collective morality, producing moral outrage. In his view, deviance is constituted only in relation to that which is not deviant: "No conception of what is morally right exists without a corresponding conception of what is morally wrong" (Hendershott, 2002: 11). From this perspective, crime and deviance serve functions for society in that they help to determine the edges and the borders of what is acceptable or unacceptable. In other words, identifying social deviance helps a society to clarify, elaborate, and maintain the boundaries of acceptability. In this regard, identifying, publicizing, and moralizing about deviance provide occasions for celebration of the social order, for the integration of groups and communities, and for "reaffirming the moral ties that bind us together" (2002: 11). For this reason, Durkheim observed that even in a society of saints there will be sinners. But we should not neglect the flip side of this argument: that making rules, setting standards, and banning behavior is also making deviance, as the relativistic social constructionists we examined earlier made clear.

A measure of social deviance then is the extent to which a behavior or an act provokes a discouraging or an indignant response. So whether a behavior is considered normal, deviant, or criminal depends on whether there is a consensus about its offensiveness, and also whether there are penalties that apply to those who engage in the behavior. However, the existence of a law, for example copyright law, does not necessarily mean it has moral authority, as the case of digital downloading or illegal song swapping shows. What is illegal does not always coincide with what is morally unacceptable, or for that matter provoke a consensus about its undesirability. Moreover, whether behavior such as digital downloading is seen as morally acceptable can vary by context and by generation. Do you, for example, consider duplicating a CD or DVD illegal? Even if it is illegal, do you consider it wrong? Suppose you borrow a DVD from a library and rip it to your computer. Is that wrong? What if you've already purchased the DVD but it got damaged and you are now just replacing what you'd already purchased? Is that wrong? What about burning a movie from the TV channel HBO onto your computer? Is that wrong? What if you are out when the movie is on, and you never worked out how to use the timed record device (who has time to do that?) and had a friend record it for you? Is that wrong? What about recording the movie that you rented from the video store (Pogue, 2007)?

Consensus about these kinds of questions varies widely across a spectrum of people in society, depending upon the perceived seriousness of the violation, and upon who is the audience making the judgment. There may well be a generational divide on this topic; young college students are far more tolerant of this kind of illegal behavior than other ages of audience. This suggests that an important factor in assessing whether a behavior is deviance or not is audience perception, and that depends not only on who is the actor, but also on who is the audience.

So, in determining what deviance is, we might wonder whether what "counts" as deviance comprises only those behaviors that offend a particularly strong and vocal interest group or whether it reflects more widely dispersed values? The expressed standards of government agencies, law enforcers, moral interest groups, local communities, sections of the media, and groups of academic commentators are involved in shaping standards against which such judgments could be made. But it is difficult to establish agreement between these different groups about what is to count as the appropriate standards, since each group has its own particular ideas and interests about what is acceptable. Is the behavior in question "societal" deviance, which refers to behavior whose condemnation is so widespread that it is shared, for the most part, in the society as a whole, or is the behavior "situational" deviance that is behavior that is problematic only in certain contexts and locales. As Goode has said, we always have to relativize deviance to a specific audience, and that audience may be the minority of a society. However, it's still deviance – *to that audience.*

To complicate matters further, in a society where people are divided into different social and professional roles, another consideration is whether what is deviant may be judged in terms of role expectations. What a doctor can do to another person because of his or her accepted role in society would get anyone else arrested for assault. The intimate sexual activities of two single people might be considered deviant if one of them was married. Here it is not the behavior itself that is deviant but the social expectations about which social roles can perform it.

Canadian sociologist and legal scholar John Hagan in his book *The Disreputable Pleasures* first proposed a helpful way out of this definitional difficulty. Hagan considers crime and deviance to be a continuous variable. He says that rule-breaking ranges from minor deviance from accepted standards of behavior, such as public rowdiness or displaying multiple body piercings, to highly offensive acts producing serious harm, such as violent terrorism or serial murder. Crime is simply a special case of deviance, one that violates "a social norm that is proscribed by criminal law" (Hagan, 1985: 49). Hagan says that, in considering offenses, we need to take account of three dimensions. First is the extent to which there is consensus or agreement about whether an act is right or wrong. Some behavior will produce a high degree of consensus concerning its wrongfulness, such as setting off a car bomb in a crowded market, killing many people. Other behavior may be considered less serious, such as the example above of downloading movies or recordings without first obtaining copyright permission. All behavior can be ranked on a scale reflecting public agreement about whether it is right or wrong. Consensus can range from high agreement that a behavior is right, through differing views or confusion about rightfulness or wrongfulness, to high consensus that it is wrong.

With regard to consensus about deviant behavior, it also matters whether the behavior is publicly known about and discussed. This, in turn, depends on the media's role in raising the issue, and on the organization of moral support behind certain issues. The media's role in deviance construction is very important and frames the ways various groups and society as a whole perceive the phenomenon. I will have more to say about this in later chapters. These influencing factors can be linked and can change over time. For example, as we saw earlier with smoking, the deviant status of this behavior has moved up on the scale of perceived harmfulness, from a behavior thought to have health-promoting effects, to one causing only personal harm, and most recently to behavior causing public harm. As the seriousness and extent of harm has increased, so too has the degree of consensus about its harmful effects and the penalties for those who participate, which have gone from segregation to fines.

A second dimension of Hagan's approach takes account of the penalties or social response imposed on an offender by society for violation. These may range from informal social ostracism or shaming, through more formal sanctions such as fines and imprisonment, to expulsion from society or incarceration, and even death. Hagan states: "The more severe the penalty prescribed, and the more extensive the support for this sanction, the more serious is the societal evaluation of the act" (1985: 49). It also matters whether or not laws or rules, and the punishments or sanctions that are embodied in them, reflect the response of society as a whole, or just those parts of society's power structure that are in control of the law-making process. For example, even though pollution of rivers or air might be a serious health hazard and affect lots of people, laws and penalties for such offenses might be relatively weak or ineffective because of lobbying of legislators by the industries affected.

Hagan's third dimension is the relative seriousness of offensive behavior based on the harm it has caused to others. Some acts, like displaying tattoos, rank low on a scale of harm to others, and might only harm the social actor (through pain, infection, or limiting career options); others, such as driving while impared from drugs or alcohol, can directly harm other people. Those that result in another's death are clearly the most harmful and, on a scale of seriousness, the most harmful would be those acts that will harm multiple others. So the seriousness of harm and the extent of harm are both important in considering this dimension. Hagan says, "the more serious acts of deviance, which are most likely to be called 'criminal,' are likely to involve: (1) broad agreement about the wrongfulness of such acts, (2) a severe social response, and (3) an evaluation of being very harmful' (1985: 50). In contrast, for many acts on the continuum there is disagreement as to their wrongfulness, an equivocal social response, and uncertainty in perceptions of their harmfulness.

In summary, what is determined to be social deviance depends on a series of shared decision making by social audiences and social actors, each deciding on what they value and what they find offensive. Behaviors are judged in relationship to the assessed seriousness and perceived extent that they cause harm to the actors or others, the degree of agreement that audiences share about this harm and the severity of the audiences' condemnation of the behavior in question, expressed through social reaction and penalties towards the offenders. Ultimately, what behaviors become designated as deviance reflects the standards and values of those groups who have the power, and occasionally the authority, to affect the location of a behavior on each of these dimensions. Social deviance, therefore, is a reflection of the power of some to define others' behavior as offensive, unwanted, and unacceptable; it is also a reflection of the forces that lead some actors to deviate and others to move back from the invitational edge.

The enduring importance of studying deviance

As a field of study, the sociology of deviance, and more recently stigma studies, has been around since the 1950s. During the past decade, Colin Sumner (1994), in his book *The Sociology of Deviance: An Obituary*, advanced the claim that the sociology of deviance was "dead." What Sumner meant was that, since the heady days of the 1960s and 1970s, there has been a decline in: (1) interest in the subject; (2) the number of deviance courses taught; (3) student enrollment in such courses; and (4) books and articles published on the topic. The essence of the "death of deviance" thesis, which was based on dubious and often anecdotal data, as we will shortly see, was that the cultural, social, and political climate of Western societies had so dramatically changed towards egalitarianism, moral tolerance, acceptance of difference, and multiculturalism, and against judging others, discrimination, and stigmatization, that the study of deviance had become redundant. Tell that to all those who suffer from mental disorders, physical disability, eating disorders, other forms of social exclusion, and they'll wonder what politically correct planet you've been living on. More importantly, tell that to the high school friends of Aqsa Parvez.

For some of these critics, the historical shift in society has been away from the disempowerment of deviants towards their empowerment. Anne Hendershott (2002), in her book *The Politics of Deviance*, thinks that this is a bad thing. Her core argument is that, in the postmodern era, social deviance has shifted from a field traditionally defined by the norms of society and elected government authority, to a field defined by politically powerful decentralized advocacy groups – such as women's groups, gay rights groups, animal rights groups – who use slick marketing and advertising techniques to persuade people, regardless of whether they want it or not, of the political correctness of their view of deviance, and who have used the notion of tolerance and moral relativity to claim the leadership in this cultural war. Hendershott contends that when control is taken from society, by which she means those in authority, the ability to morally condemn behavior, and hold actors accountable, is lost. She believes that it is necessary to reclaim the moral center from its various devolved sources in order to reaffirm the moral ties that bind us together as a society.

It is worth reflecting on whether the shifts towards what sociologists describe as late modernity or postmodernity have brought about the kind of fundamental change in social processes that these critics have suggested. The fact that some advocacy groups in the culture wars take on a politically correct attitude, critiquing those in authority who do not recognize deviance as difference, does not mean that this is a universal view. The fact that some advocacy groups can change some laws to reduce discrimination against their members does not mean those laws change permanently or that they are effective in their implementation. The fact that some interest groups can have public policy made to support their view that society should accommodate their differences does not mean that powerful forces, from hate groups moral purists, or even from the Catholic Church, are not at work seeking to condemn moral relativism and to stigmatize those who deviate from their strictures. Moreover, the fact that there have been some changes in the public discourse to be more sensitive to difference, rather than condemning it as negative deviance, does not mean that this is universally accepted, least of all in the informality of social institutional practice. A glaring example can be found in the social hierarchies of high school peers discussed in chapter 3 of this book, and the devastating effects these have on those they exclude, bully, and ridicule – and this all the time that the official position of the school and the community is not to condone bullying. That some people claim the power to exclude others, stigmatize them, and subject them to ridicule is reason enough that the subject of social deviance is worthy of study, regardless of whether a very small number of sociologists deem it a valuable enterprise.

Ironically, such claims about a subject's death usually pop up when critics are trying to replace a tried and tested concept with one of their own. In Sumner's case it was "The sociology of censure," which never caught on, although actuarial studies and analysis of the risk society, and governance through risk, did, at least in the field of criminology, if not the sociology of deviance. Over the years critics have lodged "death" claims regarding history, sociology, the Western world, and, indeed, even "the author." The fact is, as measured by books, articles, citations, and course enrollments, the field of deviance studies is as robust as ever. Consider academic citations, almost universally considered the measure of the influence of a field or discipline, scholar, article, or book. The number of papers or articles tallied published in the social sciences or humanities with "deviance" or "deviant" in the title hugely increased between the late 1950s and the 1978–82 period, then declined somewhat in the 1983–92 era. However, they then increased significantly after the early 1990s (the period in which Sumner's book was published) and have remained stable into 2007. In other words, academically, and contradictory to the clichés that critics such as Sumner and Hendershott promulgate, the field of deviance has been as vigorous and active for at least a decade and a half as it was in its so-called "glory days" of the late 1970s and early 1980s.

In addition, since the early 1990s, total enrollments and the total number of departments offering sociology of deviance courses have remained stable. Goode's (2004) research on 20 sociology department courses in sociology shows that "more departments are offering courses in deviance during any given semester than was true 30 years ago, and about the same number of students are taking the course per semester for a given department" (Goode, 2009: 566). As an indication of the national trend, enrollment in San Diego State University's (SDSU's) Sociology Department's course on deviant behavior averaged 331 students per year during the 14-year period from 1994 to 2008, and enrollment ranged from 245 to 407. Interestingly, enrollment has risen and fallen in waves. During the first wave, 1994–2003, enrollment in the course rose from a low of 245 to a high of 398 in 1997 and then fell back to a low of 283 in 2003. In the second wave, 2004–8, enrollments in deviant behavior courses rose again successively for three years to 407 in 2006 and then fell again to 334 in 2008. So it is clear, at least at this university, that the sociology of deviance is alive and well! Moreover, based on Goode's research, SDSU is no different from other universities nationwide in seeing a consistently strong interest in the subject. Indeed, he concludes that Hendershott's "claim that the field had 'died,' at least with respect to course offerings and enrollments, was *completely* false, simply a fantasy on her part" (2009: 567).

Sociologists of deviance also publish as many books and articles as they ever did and, although the field's explosion peaked in the 1980s as Goode's (2009: 572) research points out, "there were more articles published in the 1990s bearing the word 'deviance' in the title, than there were in the 1970s," and, equally significant, the rest of the field quotes those works, as was true in the past. One of the best-selling books in the entire history of sociology is Howard Becker's classic deviancy text *Outsiders* (1963). In 2009, the journal *Deviant Behavior* doubled the number of issues it publishes per year from four to eight because of the overwhelming interest in the topic. Sociologists of deviance must be doing something right because "the field seems to be going strong, with respect to both books and articles" (Goode, 2009: 572). Far from being dead, "social deviance is . . . embedded in the contesting of cultural meaning, in the media spectacle . . ." (Dotter, 2004: 286). As such, deviance cannot die, unless society dies with it.

What sociologists of deviance recognize is the foundational quality of deviance: that the study of deviance is not about a special, delimited area of social life, like medicine or sports or education or even the family – it is relevant to everyday life, it is part of everything we do, it's a general concept like stratification or power or gender or interaction; it pervades everything. In the next day or two, listen to and look at your friends and colleagues, follow them around, or hang out with some people for a whole day, watch the television or go on the web. When you do so, you'll realize that deviance is all around us, and deviance processes and issues of social control are at work in everything we do.

Summary and conclusion

In this chapter we have seen that, in considering whether behavior is social deviance, we need to examine each of the constituent components of the deviancy construction process, beginning with the audience's considerable role in deviance-making. But we also need to be aware of the reasons why some people are more likely than others to engage in deviance, and to look at what the factors are that make an actor deviant. In the study of social deviance, then, we need to explore: (1) why and how rules are made; (2) why people break rules; (3) how moral inhibition is compromised and motivation runs free; (4) the process that leads from people's behavior being taken as deviant to it coming to represent their identity; (5) how they reject, avoid, resist, manage, or accept the deviant labels conferred upon them by others; and (6) how they develop new lives, either incorporating or transcending that which others would have them be. Each of these will be themes of the subsequent chapters. As we have implied, without rules or the reactions of audiences to actors' behavior, social deviance – other than in a purely statistical sense – would not exist and would be meaningless. We turn first, then, to the question of rule-making, or banning of some kinds of behavior.

2

Why people ban behavior

In the previous chapter we saw how deviance is variously defined and how the *audience* plays a significant role in the deviance construction process. In this chapter we consider the social process involved in defining certain behavior as deviant, a process that is nothing if not political:

> The creation of deviance ... is part of a political process in which people's behavior (and/or condition) is publicly signified as different, negatively evaluated, and interpreted as violations deserving of condemnation and control. Rule-making also involves the process of defining rule violators as deviants liable to various actions allegedly designed to control them. These two features of rule-making are referred to as *banning*. (Pfuhl and Henry, 1993: 85)

Perceived differences that are negatively evaluated are the source of much banning. The difference perceived may be in behavior, ideas, or appearance. Identifying and defining a behavior draws it out from the vast array of possible behaviors as a special kind of behavior: one about which something needs to be done. Howard S. Becker, a jazz musician and sociologist, whose book *Outsiders: Studies in the Sociology of Deviance* became one of the best-selling sociology books of all time, observed:

> *Social groups create deviance by making the rules whose infractions constitute deviance* and applying those rules to particular people and labeling them outsiders. From this point of view deviance is *not* a

quality of the act a person commits but rather a consequence of the application by others of rules and sanctions to an offender. The deviant is one to whom that label has been successfully applied; deviant behavior is behavior that people so label. (Becker, 1963: 9).

Not only are behaviors seen as deviant, ideas judged to be too extreme are also banned. Communism and fascism are two obvious examples; Satanism and cult worship are others. Paranormal beliefs are deviant according to society's dominant institutions, even though widely accepted, because they challenge the view of science, and invoke a negative reaction from scientists (Goode, 2000). Indeed, "Beliefs are deviant if they fall outside the norms of acceptability and are deemed wrong, irrational, eccentric, or dangerous in a given society or by the members of a particular collectivity within a given society" (Perrin, 2007: 1140). Even within academic higher education, ideas that are deviant from an instructor's line of thinking are often subject to censure, and students have learned to be quiet in classes where they suspect the instructor is partial to either a strong left- or right-wing ideology. Consider the case of Harley Quinn, a graduate student in a large midwestern university studying for her master's degree in Marriage and Family Therapy. Her program is considered one of the best in the country and so, having a bachelor's degree from a flagship campus of the University of California (UC), Harley thought she was well suited to the challenges that a top professional program would offer. After all, being of Latino heritage, Harley had been schooled in critical social theory, particularly critical race and feminist theory, and was well versed in the issues that confronted those marginalized by institutionalized racism. Soon into the program, however, Harley found that the faculty had a particular line of thought, particularly favoring multiculturalism and integration, and the program's students either reflected it or adopted it. In either case it was a far cry from the critical thinking of her UC undergraduate education. When Harley began to interject her comments into the discussion, and share her different ideas about what created the conditions for the problems that therapists had to deal with, other students reacted. Over the course of three semesters Harley became the outcast in her classes, and seemed to offend her fellow students simply by challenging their ideas. The collective opposition to her thought resulted in hostile and controlling email from other students and complaints to the program director about Harley's offensive "behavior." This was a shock to her, but nothing like the shock she experienced when she was reprimanded and put on probation, not for poor work – she was a straight "A" student – but for saying things about institutionalized racism embedded in practices and curriculum which intimidated other students. As part of the conditions for her continuation in the program she was told that anything she said in classes and via email that other students in the program found offensive would cause her to be thrown out of the program. And this went all the way to the university's disciplinary officer who endorsed the decision. The result was extreme self-censure for fear that she would be "in trouble." Even her now minimal participation was objected to by other students who wanted her to participate in the discussions, so long as she did so in ways that affirmed their view of reality. It seems that what they really wanted was for Harley to "convert" to their way of thinking and show that she had "reformed." Not only does such treatment cause extreme stress and anxiety, and generate feelings of frustration and anger, but also it shows that even in the most mundane settings of a university educational program, "incorrect" thinking can be subject to banning and sanctioning through collective and authoritative social control.

Similarly, appearances can be banned and stigmatized. Obvious examples are people with disabilities, such as the blind, the crippled, the disfigured – like the Elephant Man – and those who wear outrageous clothes, hairstyles, or tattoos. As Heitzig points out, "appearance is a form of nonverbal communication . . . Through our appearance we identify ourselves to others and allow them to identify us":

> Of course clothing itself is a major source of symbolic meaning. Particular items of clothing, as well as cut, fabric, color, and pattern are taken as clues to the identity of the wearer. Accessories such as shoes, purses/bags, gloves, and jewelry are also part of the symbolic communication of appearance. Physical characteristics such as height, weight, muscle development, breast size, and tans are imbued with meaning as well . . . the adherence to, or violation of these informal norms of appearance allows both the wearer and the observers to make an identification of conformity or deviance. (Heitzig, 1996: 353)

Indeed, simple appearance can result in censure and attempts at control. Consider the following account of the "trouble" caused by a teen's Goth appearance:

> Most of them are dressed in black with dyed jet-black hair or a bouffant, pale skin and black make-up, regardless of sex. They go to great lengths to pick and choose their clothes. They mousse and gel their hair until it stands straight on the end and they stay out of the sun at all costs. They want to shock yet they want respect. Kelly was in McDonald's one night taking crap from a preppie university student. Her hair was a black and straggled mop. She had shocking black eyeliner and ripped black tights with some sort of black mini t-shirt.

> The cross hanging from her ear didn't help . . . The scene resulted in a
> fist fight outside the restaurant which brought the police and ended in
> arrest. How can someone's dress and appearance lead to so much
> trouble? (King, 1999: 160)

The interpretation of another's appearance as different and offensive can
lead to a reaction that seeks to control or sanction the perceived offender.
In this sense, appearance can be compared to behavior in that it has an
effect on others. When that effect is seen as negative, and applied to
children, it can be a powerful weapon in the banning process. For
example, being obese in public might be disturbing to those worried
about the rising problem of obesity. In this context, American writer
Jacob Sullum proposed:

> [b]anning fat people from public parks, where they set a bad example
> for the kids . . . Ideally, though, we should be moving toward a world
> in which no child is exposed to potential role models who normalize
> obesity and cause overeating to be approved behavior. I'm not talking
> about a complete ban on obesity. People would still be free to be fat
> in the privacy of their own homes (provided they have no children);
> they would just not be allowed to go out in public until they slimmed
> down. (Reasononline, 2001)

So, from this perspective, appearance is seen to have behavioral effects;
this is similar to banning children's access to the Internet or suppressing
their ability to view mutilated bodies. The point is that we make meaning
out of appearance, just as we do out of behavior or ideas, and if these
are viewed negatively in their effects, then we seek to ban them. Clearly,
what makes a behavior, idea, or appearance stand out as different, or
deviant, depends on the audience and their values. Whether a behavior
is banned also depends on a social process.

While we tend to think of banning as a formal process in which communities or whole societies are offended by the behavior or appearance,
most banning starts out and continues as part of an informal process by
groups of people with power and privilege; part of retaining their power
and privilege involves them policing the boundaries that separate them
from others. As an example, consider high school students in the suburban and rural United States. They are typically organized into a social
hierarchy of peers who rank themselves according to various "social
types" that include: "jocks" (good-looking athletes, football players,
wrestlers); "preppies" (who wear the latest designer fashions, are seen
as superficial yet believe they are superior to others, some of whom
become "cheerleaders"); "geeks" (technical- and computer-minded, into
sci-fi, with high IQs and no interest in sports, also known as "losers");

and "nerds" (who are thought to be super smart, read books, and are loners). Others include: dorks, dweebs, freaks, retards, gamers, goths, gangstas, and posers (for definitions and meanings of these and more see www.urbandictionary.com). The jocks and cheerleaders tend to top the high school social hierarchy in popularity and determine what behaviors are valued and what are not. The following account illustrates the social typing process at work in this former student's school, and shows how deviance and "conformity" are inextricably linked through defining who is "in" and who is "out," or who is "hot" and who is not:

> When we were in junior high school my friend Rich and I made a map of the school lunch tables according to popularity. This was easy to do because kids only ate lunch with others of about the same popularity. We graded them from A to E. A tables were full of football players and cheerleaders and so on. E tables contained the kids with mild cases of Down's Syndrome, what in the language of the time we called "retards." We sat at a D table, as low as you could get without looking physically different . . . Everyone in the school knew exactly how popular everyone else was, including us . . . I know a lot of people who were nerds in school, and they all tell the same story: there is a strong correlation between being smart and being a nerd, and an even stronger inverse correlation between being a nerd and being popular . . . teenagers are always on duty as conformists. For example, teenage kids pay a great deal of attention to clothes. They don't consciously dress to be popular. They dress to look good. But to who? To the other kids. *Other kids' opinions become their definition of right, not just for clothes, but for almost everything they do, right down to the way they walk.* And so every effort they make to do things "right" is also, consciously or not, an effort to be more popular. (Graham, 2003; my emphasis)

Those who are popular set the values that others should follow, which tend also to be shaped by prevailing socio-cultural norms about masculinity. So, in US high schools, physical strength and attractiveness are valued, as are certain kinds of style and dress. Boys also value being able to succeed in attracting good-looking female students over whom they have power. Boys who don't possess these characteristics of manly success, or behave in ways that contradict them, such as being weak in physique, having acne, studying, being obsessed with computers and technology, are excluded from the popular group's social interaction.

In later chapters I'll have more to say about the social construction of social types and stereotypes and the effects of exclusion on the excluded. Here it is important to recognize that powerful groups establish the norms and then police them by attacking, taunting, and disparaging those whose behavior or appearance is different. So what is the process that leads groups, whether high school students or citizens, to ban and condemn others' behavior, ideas, or appearance?

Banning behavior as a social process

Banning may be accomplished in the course of asserting a positive direction and intention, often to prevent health hazards and protect people from harmful consequences that might arise in the future. For example, banning may be done to protect us from human cloning or genetically altered foods, or to protect us from environmental hazards or food-borne contaminants. However, it is more common to think of banning as a reactive, rather than proactive, process. Banning is action taken by audiences against some behavior, appearance, or threat, real or imagined. Audiences are often made up of groups of unorganized people such as our high school student example. However, they can also be formed around ordinary citizens' interests or for the purpose of advocacy, as with members of residence associations, community groups, or self-help or mutual aid groups organized to lobby for their particular educational, moral, or political cause. Examples are ASH (Action on Smoking and Health), ACT UP (AIDS Coalition to Unleash Power), COYOTE (Cast Off Your Old Tired Ethics – a group organized to legalize prostitution), and NORML (National Organization for the Reform of Marijuana Laws). Such audiences are no less social types than the social types their banning actions create, as we saw with the high school example. They are people who perceive harm or feel threatened, powerless, offended, or unsettled and see banning a behavior that they find unacceptable as part of the solution to their problem. (It should be noted that, for organizations like COYOTE and NORML, their objective is *decriminalizing* a behavior they believe is acceptable since they believe the law criminalizes what they claim is victimless behavior.)

The process of banning and rule-making may begin with fear but quickly moves to a shared sense of danger and a belief among the fearful that the behavior in question is not going to go away by itself. Moreover, the problematic behavior is seen as controllable, and its control can be implemented by creating new rules, or by strengthening existing ones through extra enforcement. It is not clear why people continue to believe that rules can directly control people's behavior, especially when much of the behavior that is reacted to is already breaking norms. We'll first look at who the people are who create rules and ban behavior – called "moral entrepreneurs" – and then at how they create "moral panics" in furtherance of considering the behavior they seek to ban.

Then we'll look at the way the mass media serve as a partners in the rule-creating process.

Moral entrepreneurs

Sociologist and jazz musician Howard Becker eloquently describes the rule-making process used by audiences as being led by enterprising "moral entrepreneurs":

> Before any act can be viewed as deviant, and before any class of people can be labeled and treated as outsiders for committing the act, someone must have made the rule which defines the act as deviant. Rules are not made automatically. Even though a practice may be harmful in an objective sense to the group in which it occurs, the harm needs to be discovered and pointed out. People must be made to feel that something ought to be done about it. Someone must call the public's attention to these matters, supply the push necessary to get things done, and direct such energies as are aroused in the proper direction to get the rule created.

Deviance is a product of enterprise in the largest sense (Becker, 1963: 161). Moral entrepreneurs make rules by converting the meaning that activities have for their participants into new meanings, and by presenting these, with the help of pressure groups, through the mass media and the Internet in a way that gains the public's attention. This is usually by exaggerating an extreme form of the behavior in order to create fear and concern. An example is the banning of alcohol consumption on southern California's (and particularly San Diego's) beaches. Known as the "beach booze ban," 2008 saw the culmination of a campaign that had sought to ban drinking alcohol at the beach. As part of the social activity and beach culture in southern California, alcohol had been consumed in public for years. A growing concern by local residents, supported by restaurant and bar owners, responding to a series of what were argued to be rowdy incidents, including some folks publicly urinating in the neighborhoods surrounding the beaches, led to a campaign to ban alcohol from all beaches. The ban was supported by several prominent interest groups such as MADD (Mothers Against Drunk Driving), The San Diego County Policy Panel on Youth Access to Alcohol, and the San Diego Police Officers' Association. These groups gave the following reasons for supporting "alcohol-free beaches." Using government statistics, they claimed: "Alcohol consumption is closely linked to violence." Using local police crime data, they asserted that the Mission Beach and

Pacific Beach areas had three times the rate of violent arrests as the rest of the city and a fifth of the entire city's alcohol-related arrests. They claimed that alcohol consumption on the beaches was undermining the community and drawing excessive police resources: "Beach residents have complained of public urination, vandalism, noise, and other alcohol-related problems. Oceanside, Carlsbad, Imperial Beach, and La Jolla have banned alcohol consumption on public beaches with positive results. Law enforcement officials report a reduction in alcohol-related problems, as well as more diversity in the composition of beach crowds" (www.alcoholpolicypanel.org/beaches.shtml; site no longer active). They stated that teen parties using alcohol, presumably on the beach, were associated with a host of teen problems:

> Some consequences associated with youth alcohol problems are unwanted pregnancy, sexual assault, suicide, homicide, scholastic failure, and HIV and other STD transmission. Beaches provide appealing settings for underage drinking. The beach atmosphere is a major contributor to the drinking culture of San Diego. Allowing alcohol consumption on our beaches encourages a dangerous social norm of complacency towards underage and binge drinking. To make matters worse, police officers often cannot be certain which drinkers are and are not 21 and over. Research illustrates that *banning alcohol from beaches is an effective way to reduce alcohol-related problems, especially among youth* . . . making our local beaches alcohol-free is an example of good public policy based on a public health and safety necessity. Experience shows that once bans are in place, drunk and disorderly behavior is greatly diminished, and the beach becomes a serene and safe place where families and others can enjoy the ocean environment. *Please join law enforcement officials, community groups, and San Diego residents in making our beaches safer and healthier places to live in and visit for all!* (www.alcoholpolicypanel.org/beaches. shtml)

In the Spring of 2008, advocates of the alcohol ban appeared in newspaper columns and on local TV and radio talk shows debating the issues, with drinking advocates pointing out that earlier bans had concentrated the problems into a few areas where bans did not exist, so exaggerating them. They argued that there were already laws that governed problems associated with rowdy behavior, but to no avail. The moral entrepreneurs eventually succeeded in banning alcohol from all of San Diego's area beaches by persuading local councils to vote in favor of the ban and this was eventually supported by the passage of a Proposition celebrated by the advocacy group:

It has been a long road, and the passage of Prop D – the San Diego alcohol-free beaches initiative – is a truly momentous victory in the fight against underage and binge drinking in San Diego County . . . Our panel members, community partners, county-funded prevention providers and staff have been advocating for alcohol-free beaches for well over a decade. We encountered many obstacles along the way, including the defeat of Prop G in 2001. True social norms change takes time. If it weren't for your tireless, collective efforts over the years – mobilizing local neighborhoods and speaking to the media time and again in the face of heated public opposition – we wouldn't be here celebrating a diverse city that united to put public health and safety first. Today we can all applaud what may be the single greatest achievement in the San Diego County prevention system's coordinated efforts to change the environment in which young people gain access to and make decisions about alcohol . . . "The open bar that is the beach, is now closed." (San Diego Alcohol Policy Panel, 2009)

As we have seen, similar campaigns have been waged against smoking in public places, against assisted suicide, abortion, and drug use generally. The point here is not whether the arguments of those seeking to ban various behaviors are right or wrong, but how these interest groups marshal forces in a political campaign to bring off the resulting changes in public policy. These kinds of moral campaigns to create or change laws against certain behavior have both instrumental goals and symbolic goals. The instrumental goals are typically those stated explicitly in the campaigns, as well as some that are implicit, including, in the case of the beach booze ban, increasing restaurant and bar trade because alcohol must be consumed on licensed premises. Less obvious are the symbolic motives.

The more symbolic motive underlying rule-making activity often has to do with status conflicts between the respective supporters or defenders of the ban. Here the goal may be about establishing or underpinning a particular social group's position in the society, as Joseph Gusfield (1963) has forcefully demonstrated in the case of the early twentieth-century Prohibition laws. These laws were passed more as a status marker of middle-class Protestant Americans' demonstration of their continued dominance in the face of their fear that Irish Catholic immigrants would threaten their moral control. Smalltown Protestant America feared that rapid urbanization and Catholic immigration would undermine its economic and social position. Through the Women's Christian Temperance Movement, they pushed to have alcohol banned throughout the United States. In these kinds of cases, a change in law, or implementing a new law, may symbolize which groups are in control of the moral order of a society: "Even though it may not be enforced, merely having a law on the books reflecting one's values and interests may be taken as a measure of a group's moral stature or social status" (Pfuhl and Henry, 1993: 89). For example, analysis of the implementation of a smoking ban in Shasta County, California, shows a similar pattern to the California beach booze ban, but as the account below reveals, the ban also reflects the different economic and social status of the competing groups in the social order:

> Moral entrepreneurs crusading for the ban argued that secondhand smoke damages public health, implicitly grounding their argument in the principle that people have a right to a smoke-free environment. Status quo defenders countered that smokers have a constitutional right to indulge wherever and whenever they see fit . . . The moral entrepreneurs who engineered the smoking ban campaign were representatives of the prestigious knowledge class, including among their members officials from the local chapters of respected organizations at the forefront of the national anti-smoking crusade. In contrast the small business owners, who were at the core of the opposing coalition of status quo defenders, represented the traditional middle class. Clearly there was an instrumental quality to the restaurant and bar owners' stance, because they saw the ban as potentially damaging to their business interests . . . In many respects, the status conflicts involved in the Shasta County smoking ban were symbolic . . . Ultimately, a lifestyle associated with the less educated, less affluent, lower occupational strata was stigmatized as a public health hazard and targeted for coercive reform. Its deviance status was codified in the ordinance banning smoking in public facilities, including restaurants and bars. The ban symbolized the deviant status of cigarette smokers, the prohibition visibly demonstrating the community's condemnation of their behavior. Further the smoking ban symbolically amplified the purported virtues of the abstinent lifestyle. (Tuggle and Holmes, 2006: 158).

Whether it is instrumental or symbolic, the conversion of some groups' private moralities into public issues is necessary if their concern is to gain sufficient legitimacy to warrant more formal rule-making. In this process, a principal partner is the media. They can act either as a forum for the display of concern or as an instrument for agitating it, as we shall see later in this chapter.

Clearly the range of strategies for mobilizing public moral support is as wide as that available to candidates in a political campaign. Moral entrepreneurs can promote their case for a behavioral ban by associating their proposed rules with positive values or benefits to society. Particularly popular are those bans claimed to increase health or freedom. A similarly powerful impact can be achieved by associating the continued existence of questioned behavior with negative values, pointing up its threat to the mental, physical, or moral fabric of organized society. Groups of moral entrepreneurs can draw respectability from the public by establishing alliances with respected members of society or by recruiting these people's testimonies, if not their person. Any endorsement by public officials takes the rule-making case towards a complete ban. Any myth-making, which can be employed to exaggerate aspects of the behavior or to help hang the activity on the backs of already recognized undesirable social types, will help their cause. The strategy of creating "moral panic" and of demonizing sections of the population is also used and can be based on fact or myth.

The creation of moral panics

British sociologist Stanley Cohen (1972), in his *Folk Devils and Moral Panics*, coined the term "moral panic." Cohen described the demonization through the mass media around the 1960s "Mods" and "Rockers," teen rebel groups whose behavior was claimed to threaten valued British cultural norms. In general, moral entrepreneurs promote the idea that particular groups in the population are "folk devils" doing evil, regardless of whether any serious harm exists. According to Erich Goode and Norman Ben-Yehuda (1994) in *Moral Panics: The Social Construction of Deviance*, moral panics are societal reactions to perceived threat that have certain characteristics. They have volatility and a life cycle in which they suddenly appear in the media, rapidly spread among large sections of the population, and then just as rapidly decline in further appearances of the problem. One example is the 1980s panic around US private day care providers who, it was claimed, were engaging in "satanic ritual child abuse" and who "were abusing their very young charges in satanic rituals that included such practices as blood-drinking, cannibalism, and human sacrifices" (de Young, 2006: 163; 1997). These accusations began in 1983 and ended in 1991 and involved over 100 day care centers nationwide, whose staff were investigated, charged, and in many cases convicted and given long prison sentences.

An important issue in considering the rule-creation process is how interest groups, moral entrepreneurs, and social movements create claims about the behavior that they consider to be deviant. Criminologist Ray Surette describes how this "claims making" works.

> Claims-makers are the promoters, activists, professional experts and spokespersons involved in forwarding specific claims about a phenomenon. Social problems emerge – become a focus for concern – through a process of claims making. The process determines not only which phenomena come to be designated as social problems, but which characteristics are ascribed to those problems. Claims-makers do more than draw attention to a particular social condition, they shape our sense of what the problem is. Each social condition can be constructed as many different social problems ... and each construction implies different policy courses and solutions. The social roles and ideologies of claims-makers affect their characterization of problems; where moralists see sin, medical authorities detect disease, and criminal justice personnel see crime. (Surette, 1998: 8–9)

Claims making, then, not only occurs at particular historical moments, but also involves, first, a process of assembling claims about behavior or conditions seen as morally problematic. Second, it involves presenting these claims as legitimate to significant audiences, not least through the news media. In this process claims makers can gain more traction for the veracity of their claim if the questioned behavior is tied to other issues of concern. So, in the alleged day care sexual abuse example, the linkage was made to Satanism. In the alcohol-free beach campaign, the issue was tied to teenage suicide, sex, and HIV-AIDS. Third, a key task in framing a moral problem involves the prognosis of how to address the problem in order to bring about a desired outcome, by defining strategies, tactics, and policy. Fourth, claims making involves contesting counter claims and mobilizing the support of key groups.

Erich Goode and Norman Ben-Yehuda say that moral panics also gain public legitimacy through the emergence of experts who claim to be authorities in discerning cases of the said feared behavior. In the case of satanic ritual abuse, this group of "experts" was comprised of social workers and mental health professionals, who claimed to be able to identify the satanic menace by reframing the words of children as young as two years of age into accusations against their providers, as well as against others including business people, politicians, and family members (de Young, 2006: 165). These professionals' claims to expertise were bolstered by attorneys and law enforcement officials and were supported by a newly generated body of materials. Mary de Young describes the process:

> Professionals developed and widely disseminated a wholly synthetic diabolism out of materials haphazardly borrowed from eclectic sources on Satanism, the occult, mysticism, paganism and witchcraft ... They

constructed "indicator lists" to assist other professionals . . . in identifying child victims, and "symptom lists" to guide the course of their
therapy . . . a burgeoning critical literature was deeply dividing the
professional field into claims-makers and counterclaims makers,
believers and skeptics. (de Young 2006: 166–7)

Following the initial revelations, a moral panic spreads by an increased
identification of cases of the behavior that build into a "wave"; in the
case of satanic ritual abuse, accusations began at one California pre-
school and spread to over 100 child care facilities nationwide. The news
was spread via local news media's sensational coverage of the latest
"revelations," supported by the "experts" who appeared on television
talk shows and news magazines and testified as expert witnesses at
trials. Joining them were the parents of the allegedly victimized children,
some of whom formed anti-child abuse interest groups such as
Citizens Against Child Abuse, Believe the Children and CLOUT (which
lobbied for children to be allowed to testify as witnesses in criminal
trials).

Moral panics like this one produce an intense hostility towards the
accused, who are seen as enemies of society. As enemies, they are then
persecuted. In the alleged child abuse example, this resulted in public
vilification via the media and convictions by the courts resulting in long
prison sentences. Moral panics also feature systems to assess the moral
feeling of the public consensus about the seriousness of the threat. In
moral panics there is typically a disproportional fear relative to actual
harm caused. Indeed, Jeffrey Victor's study of this child abuse, reported
in *Satanic Panic* (1993; 1998), shows that moral panics need not be
based in reality, but can be constructed on the basis of imaginary deviants whose existence gains credibility in the eyes of the public when
authorities, and those who claim expert knowledge – particularly of
science or medicine – legitimize the accusations. Moreover, these panics
are likely to occur when competing bureaucratic agencies are vying for
jurisdiction of authority, when methods of detection result in errors, and
when there is a symbolic resonance with a perceived threat identified in
a prevailing demonology – which serves as a master cognitive frame that
organizes problems, gives meaning to them, explains them, and offers
solutions.

Finally, moral panics tend to unravel when a backlash against the
persecution occurs; and when exposure of the flaws in identifying the
problem begins to emerge. In the child abuse case described above,
the critics had exposed major flaws in the process and accounts had
silenced its most vocal advocates (Victor, 1993). Other factors contributed to the death of the panic, including changes in the number of women

in the workforce, changes in day care licensing, and changes in day care operations, including installing video cameras and making them more open and accessible (de Young, 2006: 167–8; de Young, 1997). In the end, many of the charges against alleged offenders were dropped and previous convictions were overturned on appeal. Overall, the phenomenon of moral entrepreneurs creating moral panics to establish rules and laws to control what they see as undesirable behavior depends on their ability to make credible claims, and that too is a political process. The mass media play a significant role in the process of moral conversion.

Mass media and public policy

Ray Surette has pointed out that the relationship between mass media and social culture is reciprocal, with each affecting the other:

> As the distributors of social knowledge, the media also legitimize people, social issues, and social policies for the general public. And though the media do not control the process of cultural change, the fact is that in large industrialized nations with hundreds of millions of people, cultural change without media involvement does not occur. The media simultaneously change, react to and reflect culture and society. (Surette, 1998: 11)

Competing claims about a social issue or problematic behavior are played out in the mass media. Crime and deviance comprise a large part of television and popular culture, where they are used not only to inform, as in "news," but also as a source of entertainment (Altheide, 2007: 1107). Some of the most popular shows on television are crime, police or court dramas such as *The Sopranos, Law and Order, CSI, Boston Legal, Bones,* and *Criminal Minds,* etc. This is the forum in which claims makers compete for the public's attention. However, the media themselves are a collection of competing interest groups, particularly the news media, each vying for the top stories and using the tried and tested formula that "if it bleeds, it leads." Indeed, news media and television, especially local news media, are interested in dramatic claims and sensational stories about problems and issues related to major cultural tropes. As a result, not all news is covered; news editors filter out some news and promote other news. Without powerful or organized sponsors, and without journalistic ties, it is difficult to break into the media. Organizations that form around public issues must develop a public relations specialty that nurtures media relations and establishes channels for news releases and expert sources. Part of the job of these interest groups is to manage the quality of their media exposure, particularly with regards to including or excluding critical facts, and by a variety of strategies including presentational style:

> Of particular importance is how information is presented, e.g., the sequencing of contradictory positions, the amount of coverage each is given, and the orientations of those reporting the "facts." By altering these elements, the image and the desired definition (meaning) of an issue may be affected. Further, by varying visual and auditory stimuli it is possible to increase or decrease the likelihood that an audience will perceive a situation to be consistent with or contradictory to recognized standards or principles . . . Legitimacy may also be generated by careful use of emotionally loaded words or images, and selectively linking a cause with (or disassociating it from) existing positive values . . . In addition to aligning their own aims with positive values, moral entrepreneurs try to denigrate the opposition by linking it with negative values. (Pfuhl and Henry, 1993: 95)

This manipulation of the media by powerful interest groups supported by, and facilitated through, spin-doctors, is designed to shape public policy to reflect the views of these groups, as Ray Surette notes: "Policies and solutions sought are tied to the claims of the successful winning construction. The linking of claims to policies involves claims makers who often describe a social problem in a simplified, dramatic, worst-case scenario launching media-based moral crusades and panics. The claims influence the formation of social policy and the solutions that are seen as workable" (Surette, 1998: 11). Indeed, in his comprehensive analysis of *Media, Crime and Criminal Justice*, Surette (1998) summarizes the key findings on the role that mass media play in creating public policy. He says that the news and entertainment media's impact on the public's conception of crime is difficult to predict and has uncertain effects on various claims makers. However, more convincing evidence exists about "agenda building." Research supports the view that the greatest impact the media make is on raising the *fear* of crime among the population, and shaping criminal justice policy. Surette argues that models of the effects of mass media campaigns on the general public shifted from the 1930s view that the media was a "Hypodermic needle-like mechanism that could be used to inject information and attitudes directly into the public" to a view in the 1950s and 1960s that the media merely reinforced pre-existing views held by members of the public. By the 1970s the view emerged that the media's impact was affected by social factors and social demographics, including the notion that who viewed what kind of media had an effect on whether they were influenced by its messages. Although the media's effect was still strongest in reinforcing and strengthening existing attitudes, the new research also suggested that the mass media could: (1) form attitudes where the topic was new to the public; (2) change attitudes where attitudes were weakly held; (3) strengthen some attitudes relative to others; (4) change strongly held attitudes with new facts; and (5) suggest new responses and policy directions (1998: 200).

The important point for our purposes in this chapter is that the mass media's impact is seen to be greatest in generating citizen awareness and attitudes about new problems, precisely the kind of awareness and attitude that moral entrepreneurs were intent on generating. Surette says there are three areas of importance. The first is the role of the media in raising the significance of crime as a public issue, relative to other issues, which is called "agenda setting." It appears that the linear model of the media influencing public policy is not supported by the research. In other words, it is not the case that the media creates a story on an issue, "the issue increases in importance to the public, the public becomes alarmed, interest groups mobilize, and policy makers respond" (1998: 202).

The second area of importance is shaping the public's beliefs and attitudes about crime, called "agenda building," which resonates with the activities of moral entrepreneurs, and seems to have more research support. Here an interactive reciprocal effect occurs between the media and policy makers, such that fear of crime victimization disproportionate with the real level of harm "encourages moral crusades against specific crime issues, heightens public anxiety about crime, and pushes or blocks other serious problems . . . from the public agenda" (1998: 203).

The third significant area is the media's influence on criminal justice policy. Given the strong empirical connection between the fear of criminal victimization and mass media influences, moral entrepreneurs who emphasize and exaggerate the fear of crime have an obvious and clear strategy to bring about changes in policy. This is particularly the case in the criminalizing of new harms about which the public has little knowledge:

> Effects on policy are therefore the ultimate prize in the construction of crime and justice reality competition. Claims-makers forward their competing crime-and-justice claims in an effort to steer the social construction of crime-and-justice policy gaining power, resources, and credibility in the process . . . Recent research does suggest that the news media . . . significantly affect policy preferences among the public for general social issues. The content of television news broadcasts favoring or opposed to specific policies consequently shifts public opinion in the same direction as the news coverage . . . researchers generally

interpret the association as part of a causal chain that results in real-world changes in public support for policies that are reported favorably in the broadcast or print media. Recognizing this, claims-makers work diligently to garner media attention and favor. (1998: 213)

The relationship between claims makers, public opinion and public policy is conceived, therefore, not so much as a linear causal one but more as an ecological reciprocal one in which the mass media are themselves "claims making actors in the politics of policy formation." In other words, the media shape criminal justice policy "by establishing ongoing relationships with other local claims-makers including policy makers, lobbyists and public officials" (1998: 214). This process involves journalists collaborating with officials and policy makers, each of whom co-produce policy outcomes and can and do choose to draw on the cases that moral entrepreneurs bring before them and that resonate with their own policy aspirations.

It is important here to point out the changing form of news and entertainment, which has increasingly become integrated around the Internet and hand-held phones such as Apple's iPhone and the Blackberry. Some newspapers have moved from print to fully online (e.g. the *Christian Science Monitor*), and others have been launched only online (e.g. the *Voice of San Diego*). Regardless of the shift in form, these new organizations still rely on links through reporters to influential experts, and the *process* of making the news to change ideas, views or policy towards banning behavior is as we have described it in this chapter. Ironically, the Internet itself has also become a subject for moral panic, as some moral entrepreneurs want it banned or controlled to stop children having access to pornography or extremist ideas.

From banning behavior to making laws

Ultimately, of course, the goal of banning a behavior will be met if the powers of the state can be "captured," such that laws are passed criminalizing the behavior in question. This will empower the major law enforcement agencies to act, in the name of the whole society, on behalf of those groups with immediate concerns. At this point, the interest group can be said to have established an official ban against the behavior. To accomplish this, moral entrepreneurs need to use power. So far we have been largely using behavior as an example of the banning process, and it might seem too far-fetched to consider the banning of appearance. How can appearance be banned? Can laws be enacted to ban appearance? Well, this was tried in Mississippi where the House Bill 282, sponsored by Representative Mayhall, a retired pharmaceutical sales-man, made it to the Mississippi State House in January 2008. The pro-posed law would have banned restaurants from serving people with a BMI (Body Mass Index) higher than 30 (for example, for a person of 5 ft 9 ins. tall, this would be anyone over 203 lb). Under the bill, res-taurants would be monitored for compliance by the State Department of Health and those found in violation of the law would have their business permits revoked:

State of Mississippi

HOUSE BILL NO. 282

An act to prohibit certain food establishments from serving food to any person who is obese, based on criteria prescribed by the State Department of Health; to direct the department to prepare written materials that describe and explain the criteria for determining whether a person is obese and to provide those materials to the food establish-ments; to direct the department to monitor the food establishments for compliance with the provisions of this act; and for related purposes. Be it enacted by the legislature of the state of Mississippi:

SECTION 1.
(1) The provisions of this section shall apply to any food establishment that is required to obtain a permit from the State Department of Health under Section 41-3-15(4)(f), that operates primarily in an enclosed facility and that has five (5) or more seats for customers.
(2) Any food establishment to which this section applies shall not be allowed to serve food to any person who is obese, based on criteria prescribed by the State Department of Health after consultation with the Mississippi Council on Obesity Prevention and Management estab-lished under Section 41-101-1 or its successor. The State Department of Health shall prepare written materials that describe and explain the criteria for determining whether a person is obese, and shall provide those materials to all food establishments to which this section applies. A food establishment shall be entitled to rely on the criteria for obesity in those written materials when determining whether or not it is allowed to serve food to any person.
(3) The State Department of Health shall monitor the food establish-ments to which this section applies for compliance with the provisions of this section, and may revoke the permit of any food establishment that repeatedly violates the provisions of this section.

SECTION 2. This act shall take effect and be in force from and after July 1, 2008.

If law is not the outcome of a banning process, "captured institutions" such as science, religion, education, and public opinion are a significant creative accomplishment in the social construction of deviance. But it must not be forgotten that all of these institutions and agencies are themselves groups with interests and they may divide on the issue, depending whether these interests are advanced or threatened by the existence of a particular proposed ban. At the very least such groups are likely to graft their interests onto the proposed ban such that what emerges is some compromise position, not necessarily the one that the original advocates had in mind.

Not surprisingly, the chances of resisting the ban are considerably improved if those engaged in the behavior, or those who wish to see us remain free to choose it, engage in a counter political campaign. In this context, controversy, rather than consensus, can be claimed. In such circumstances, the law becomes a weapon in the battle between competing interest groups and can actually create conflict by being a resource to be won.

In this chapter we have seen that rules are created to ban behavior based on an audience's selection of what it finds different and offensive. Audiences can be informally organized social cliques or more powerfully organized official interest/advocacy groups. In either case, they enforce their view of what is acceptable or unacceptable. In the case of informal groups, this can occur through a hierarchy of domination and exclusion. For more organized groups, it involves a political process of escalation that moves a private problem to a public issue. Moral entrepreneurs mobilize the mass media and public officials to create public interest in their claim through moral panic and fear of harm, with the objective of banning the behavior, preferably through enacting law. In the next chapter, we will see what motivates people to behave in ways that others find offensive.

3

Why some people break rules: from extreme to mundane deviance

It's Friday night at the Golden Bow . . . Before the bar gets busy, the dancers hang out in the bathroom . . . The girls who do drugs hang together. Laura doesn't really "hang" with anyone because of the drugs she does. Her high involves needles. She smokes crack, coke, and pot and tops it off with Southern Comfort. This kind of mixed high is not unusual for this bar . . . Drug use is not limited to the dancers. Some of the waitresses do them too . . . Selling drugs in this bar is easy. You can recognize the players. They are the ones the girls talk to. After talking they go to the bathroom for a short time . . . Most of the dancers and waitresses have a drinking problem, at least while they are at work. There are two basic reasons why they get high on drink and drugs. One is to get the courage to get up on stage and the other is to deal with the kind of people we get in here . . . About the time the bar starts to get busy, the waitresses and dancers are feeling "good" and ready to go to work. The other dancers begin showing up. These are the ones only working for the tips they get while dancing. The dancers that were here at the start of the night have already found some customers to sit with them, who will buy them a drink and who will tip them too. It is at this time that some of the sex acts take place . . . between customers and dancers and waitresses. They can range from putting dollar bills down a girl's shirt or G-string (to get a quick feel) to sitting there with the girl with his hands between the upper parts of her legs. "Lap dances" are another way of providing sex acts for money. In a lap dance, the dancer literally dances in your lap, often fondling and rubbing you with her hands and body. There are no limits. Chrissy is doing lap dances. It's really sex: the guy paid her one hundred dollars to have sex with him. Chrissy gets on this guy's lap and starts to grind. This turns him on. He tips more money for more action . . . Sue is one of the dancers. I asked her to explain some of the activities: "Drug use is common because it helps a person deal with the customers. The sale of drugs is hard for a dancer to do" . . . When I asked if there are pressures from other dancers to get involved in drug use and sex she said "Yes, if you don't join in and do what the others do, they keep pushing until you feel weird." I asked her what she would not do: "Slutting . . . The guys are not called 'tricks' they are called 'friends.' You don't hook for money, but rather you go out with a friend and make extra money." . . . Some of the dancers, on their nights off, walk the streets and prostitute . . . "Not all of the dancers are streetwalkers but all are some sort of hooker" . . . I asked if there is anything that she hates about the type of job that she does . . . she hates the kind of men that come in here: "They are ass-holes. But even so I'll take their money and listen to their bullshit" . . . I found that the major motive was the money that can be earned. Given the limited hours and the skills that the dancers have (Sue dropped out of high school when she was 15), this is a way to make good money. "I don't know any other way to make a living . . . so I make the best of what I've got." A related motive is drugs. They work all night just to go spend it all on drugs . . . The cycle is endless and hard to break. Some girls seek help to break this cycle only to return and get right back into the pattern from which they just escaped. But there are often deeper reasons in these girls' lives that are part of any explanation for what they do. Many of them come from broken homes. Their home life is full of abuse. Many of the girls are forced into prostitution either by their boyfriends, or by their spouse. In most cases the girls are subject to physical, as well as mental abuse at home. When they come to work, this is the time of their day that men are not hurting them. Dancing is their way of getting love and tenderness – even though it is artificial and temporary. Sue explains, "The person up on stage is not really me, but my twin sister. The customers are not really there. The guy deserves to be taken advantage of or he would not be there." (Shaw, 1999: 36–40)

In this chapter we consider the elusive question of why some people deviate from social norms. The underlying assumption is that everyone deviates to some degree in some behaviors. The ironic fact is that to be a total conformist is statistically deviant, as studies of honesty and dishonesty reveal. Behavior is distributed along a normal curve with most people's behavior being within an acceptable range or distance from the norm. However, some people's behavior deviates significantly from the norm and the questions are why and, in particular, how they come to participate in it.

Another way of looking at this question is the reverse: Why do people conform? If the answer to this question is that people conform because of effective socialization and social pressure, this leads to the further question of what it is about the process of socialization that fails, leading some people to deviate? Also important is what happens when those who raise children, whether parents or surrogates, are themselves deviant, such that the children are socialized into deviance as normality. In this chapter, we will explore how and by what mechanism those who are socialized to conformity have that commitment to conventional behavior eroded to the point of complete suspension, or at least to a level of ambiguity. We will also look at the failure of others to form a significant commitment to conformity in the first place.

As can be seen from our opening example, what is normal and what is conformity depends on the context. As an activity, exotic dancing could be considered a deviant form of work, yet it is legal and relatively commonplace in cities in the USA. Even where a set of behavior is itself considered deviant from society's norms, some people's behavior is deviant within the norms of that deviance. Conformity in the strip bar among exotic dancers focuses around a range of legal drinking, illegal drug behavior and sex acts, yet some dancers and waitresses go beyond even these local norms, engaging in additional deviant behavior described as "slutting" or prostitution; others may do an excessive amount of drugs not only defined by law as illegal but also seen locally among the dancers as deviant: in this situational context, it is normal to use alcohol and pot and even cocaine, but any drug use involving needles is seen as deviant. Research on strippers' lifestyles also suggests that lesbian/gay activity is not uncommon because of the emotional isolation from affective social relationships, unsatisfactory relationships with males, and an opportunity structure allowing a variety of sexual behavior. Whether they have problems in their marital relations or have suffered abuse by men at home:

> The men with whom strippers have the most frequent contact are those in their audience, unattached men that they define as "degenerate" . . . Added to this is the presence of lesbians among strippers and the warm reception strippers are likely to receive from those who frequent gay bars where they sometimes go for relaxation. Taken together this complex of elements serves to promote a negative definition of the relationships with men, and a positive definition of relationships with women, meanings that are consistent with these women's willingness to enter into a lesbian relationship. (Pfuhl and Henry, 1993: 56).

In this chapter we will look at rule-breaking and deviant behavior as a process that involves an interrelated set of factors that lead otherwise conventional people to make deviant choices. I will examine the factors that facilitate their choices and at the ways in which any moral qualms people may have are removed, ultimately revealing their motives. That people are motivated to choose certain behavior which others define as deviant is not to say that they freely choose it, nor that they are driven to it, as we shall see in what follows.

Deviance as a social process

Rather than being forced into deviant acts or deviant lifestyles or even deviant careers, most people have a choice about whether or not to break rules or act in ways that others might find offensive. But that choice is not completely free. It is both limited and facilitated by various biological, psychological, situational, relational, institutional, structural, and cultural constraints. We humans exercise *limited* rational free choice. Our choices are shaped and channeled by our circumstances and the contexts in which we find ourselves. We exist in a series of meaningful environments, but the meaning these have for us varies depending upon our biography and our role in the socio-cultural environment that we inhabit. Consider a school. It has the same classrooms and labs, theatre facilities, libraries and computer equipment, play areas and athletics fields for both teachers and students. For teachers, it is their work place, established to teach students subjects that they learned at college and university; to inspire students to learn and to go on to become engaged citizens with career opportunities and choices and a professional identity in the community. For students, as we saw in the previous chapter, it *can* be these things, but it can also be more powerfully a source of social hierarchy, a place of cliques and social dominance controlled by popular students to their advantage. To those excluded from the "in" group, it can be seen as a place of terror. As one former student comments on his understanding of the meaning of American junior high schools:

> [T]hey were just holding pens . . . their primary purpose is to keep kids locked up in one place for a big chunk of the day so adults can get things done . . . When I was in school, suicide was a constant topic among the smarter kids. No one I knew did it, but several planned to, and some may have tried. Mostly this was just a pose. Like other teenagers, we loved the dramatic, and suicide seemed very dramatic. But partly it was because our lives were at times genuinely miserable . . . Bullying was only part of the problem. Another problem, and

possibly an even worse one, was that we never had anything real to work on. Humans like to work; in most of the world, your work is your identity. And all the work we did was pointless or seemed so at the time ... At best it was practice for real work we might do far in the future ... More often it was just an arbitrary series of hoops to jump through, words without content designed mainly for testability. (The three main causes of the Civil War were. ... Test: List the three main causes of the Civil War.) ... And there was no way to opt out. The adults had agreed among themselves that this was to be the route to college. The only way to escape this empty life was to submit to it. (Graham 2003)

As social actors, we are embedded in networks of meaning (or meaninglessness) and our biographical development is tied to the meaning that social institutions have in the wider society. But what we understand about these institutions also reflects the meaning that we make through relations with each other in that society. Our biography

consists of the highly individualized and variable circumstances, events and their changing meanings that constitute individual social and moral careers ... Biography is ... a compound of fragmented experiences and conditions woven into a life. As they are constructed and confronted, defined and responded to by the actor, such individually unique and endlessly varied experiences are the social fabric of meaning in a complex society. (Pfuhl and Henry, 1993: 54)

Humans accumulate experiences and selectively look back, making them meaningful in the context of their present life: "People's biography is what they perceive it to be from their present standpoint" (1993: 54). In order to illustrate the interrelationship between these individual biographical elements and environmental elements, let's consider an example of extreme deviance: the case of school violence – particularly, the rampage school shootings that took place in the United States (and other nations) during the late 1990s, and continue episodically today. Extreme deviance illustrates in vivid ways the interconnectedness between biography and environment that is characteristic of more mundane deviance.

Rampage school shootings as extreme social deviance

Rampage school shootings are both statistically and criminally extremely deviant. That is, they are exceptional statistically in that they are very rare, and they are sites of mass or multiple, almost random, homicide, which is on the extreme negative end of the deviance continuum. The evidence suggests that, in the United States, the perpetrators of these offenses are typically male teenagers from intact families living in normal suburban and rural communities. These extreme deviant acts of mass murder are the culmination of a series of interrelated processes, operating at several levels in society beyond the unique characteristics of those individuals ultimately caught up in the culminating drama; the wider socio-cultural environmental meanings become embodied in the individual biographies of those involved. As sociologist Katherine Newman and her colleagues, who conducted one of the most extensive studies of the phenomenon, state in *Rampage: The Social Roots of School Shootings*, "any particular episode arises from multiple causes interacting with one another . . . at the individual, community and national levels . . . Take away any one of these elements, and the shootings . . . would not have happened" (Newman et al., 2004: 229). They further state:

> Based on our research . . . we propose five necessary but not sufficient conditions for rampage school shootings . . . The first necessary factor is the shooter's perception of himself as extremely marginal in the social worlds that matter to him. Among adolescents, whose identities are closely tied to peer relations and positions in the pecking order, bullying and other forms of social exclusion are recipes for marginalization and isolation, which in turn breed extreme levels of desperation and frustration. Second, school shooters must suffer from psychosocial problems that magnify the impact of marginality. [Third] "Cultural scripts" – prescriptions for behavior – must be available to lead the way toward an armed attack . . . The shooter must believe that unleashing an attack on teachers and classmates will resolve his dilemmas . . . The fourth necessary factor is failure of surveillance systems that are intended to identify troubled teens before their problems become extreme. Finally . . . a school shooting cannot occur unless a youth can obtain unsupervised access to a weapon. (2004: 229–30)

Examination of the perpetrators of rampage school shootings reveals that one factor, or one set of factors, was operative at the individual level, possibly biological in origin and certainly psychological in manifestation. In a biological sense, these extreme deviants possessed physical looks that were either unattractive or physically puny. They were males variously described as "small, skinny or overweight, with glasses and sometimes acne, and usually nerdy, awkward and withdrawn. Very few of these boys seem to meet the physical and social ideals of masculinity – tall, handsome, muscular, athletic, and confident" (2004: 242). Based in part on these biological qualities, these boys were consistently and repeatedly excluded from popular peer group cultures. As a result of continual negative peer interaction, such as being repeatedly ridiculed or bullied, they developed psychological problems. Over time, these may also combine with, or magnify, pre-existing psychological problems such as low self-esteem and a sense of worthlessness. A US Government Center for Disease Control (CDC) study, for example, found that "three quarters of the offenders felt persecuted, bullied, threatened, or had been subject to attack or injury by others prior to a rampage shooting." A 1999 FBI report, *Lessons Learned*, found that rampage school shooters had low self-esteem, felt rejected, experienced themselves as different, experienced self-loathing, felt powerless, and sought recognition. They were also shown to have had a history of depression, and four out of five had experienced suicidal/homicidal ideation. The CDC data reveal that between 20 and 50 percent of shooters had suffered some form of mental disorder. Thus, clearly, psychological factors combine with biological ones and, through social interaction, shape the meaning of a person's life. These psychological conditions are highly related to the abuse these students received from their peers. A study on types of victims and victimization reveals that, while some adapt and cope resiliently with these adverse conditions, others withdraw and experience reduced self-esteem and diminished social self-efficacy: "Yet, others may react to these affronts by seeking to 'level the score' and by taking revenge or retribution . . . Insidiously, the last response can lead to a chronic perpetration–retribution cycle that has no easy or clear exit" (Furlong, Sharma, and Rhee, 2000: 83).

Clearly, parental influence can offset exclusion by peers, but these students experienced a perceived lack of family support and had problems with their parents. For example, Newman's study (Newman et al., 2004: 245) found that 85 percent of the shooters came from dysfunctional homes, were suicidal, or depressed, or suffered from a major mental disorder. Moreover, asking for help from parents was likely seen as an inappropriate choice, given that "real men" don't ask for help. It was also unlikely to be an easy question to ask of the school that allowed this abusive behavior to continue.

For those students who reacted to their humiliation and perceived pain, there were several choices they confronted in dealing with their unpleasant situation. They could ignore it and carry on; however, "bullying and exclusion, tolerable to adolescents who learn to live with it, become impossible volcanic pressures" among students plagued by psychological problems (2004: 242–3). Alternatively, they could find friends of their own and stay away from trouble, which many did. But often the friends they found reinforced their view of the problems. Most of those who became school shooters had friends who "tended to come from the outcast cliques like the Trench Coat Mafia (at Columbine) or the Goths (at Heath)" (2004: 239). They could try to escape their lowly position in the school social hierarchy by adopting an accepted social role, such as "class clown," as did some shooters, for example Kip Kinkle, who killed his parents and two students and shot 20 others. As Newman and her colleagues say, these attempts by troubled teens to change their social position in the school hierarchy fail because the students in question often don't have the required social skills, which makes them vulnerable to even more ridicule. But they do have choices, albeit diminishing and unrealistic ones.

Alternatively, those victimized by a series of abuses from their peers could justifiably react against those who assaulted them. A study on school fighting found that 84 percent of youths justified their violent interactions by arguing that they were retaliating against harm to themselves, or reacting to others' offensive or insulting behavior, or acting in self-defense, or helping a friend who had been attacked (Lockwood, 1997). However, for those who do not react immediately, because they are not brave enough or physically strong enough, or who are not confident enough, and who instead allow their negative feelings to build up over time, there was a danger of their inner torment turning to anger and rage against those students who abused them, against their parents for being unable to protect them, and against the community symbolized through the school.

While they still had diminishing perceived choices, the availability of culturally provided solutions to their problem was also a factor. As Newman et al. say:

> It is a mistake to think of shooters as impulsive or erratic, for they are virtually the opposite. They ruminate on their difficulties, consider a variety of options – though generally to no effect – and then decide on shooting as a last resort. The decision is not random, though. It is a consequence of cultural scripts that are visible in popular culture . . . For School shooters . . . scripts that connect manhood to guns, domination, and the power that comes from terrifying the innocent, offer a template for action. Books, TV, movies and song lyrics influence decisions that direct their anger outward instead of inward; they provide the justification for random attacks. They are a set of stage directions. (2004: 246, 253)

Many students involved in incidents of rampage shooting were found by the FBI report to enjoy violent media messages in certain songs, movies, or video games. Many of them had read satanic or cult works, listened to violent songs, and were obsessed by reports of other school shootings.

This media and popular cultural imagery is exploited by the commercial music industry through rap and hip-hop culture that is often misogynistic and hateful, and feeds into the alienation and anger of youth. It is captured in heavy-metal rock and Goth culture, which in the case of Columbine allowed the perpetrators, Eric Harris and Dylan Klebold, to express their feelings of rage and alienation. At this point, all that is needed are the weapons and the ability to defeat social control and detection mechanisms.

National policies on gun ownership and sales make available the means for those with a grudge to exercise power over others and to "level the score." Important, too, as Philip Larkin has pointed out, is a pervasive gun culture combined with a paramilitary culture, "that culminated in the bombing of the federal building in Oklahoma City" (Larkin, 2007: 196). He says that the "culture of celebrity in postmodern America" glorifies notoriety and fame, such that, through these broad societal cultural themes, the specific modalities of video games, television, rock music, adolescent subcultures, and mental disorder can be considered meaningful. So, with motivation, justification, and available cultural scripts, the "manly choice" to "right the wrongs" through a dramatic exit of violence seemed like the rampage shooter's only solution to the torment they had experienced.

In the end, these extreme deviants still had a few, albeit ever-diminishing, choices, but they were increasingly unable to see any alternatives beyond the violent ones that loomed large in their narrowing worldview. Indeed, school shooters commonly face a feeling of "being trapped and needing a 'manly' exit from an unbearable situation . . . They want to die to end their torment." School shooters either kill themselves during the shooting event, or hope that police will kill them in the process: "Virtually no one ever gets away with a rampage shooting, and most everyone who commits this type of crime is aware of that." And so, in their final acts, these teenage boys commit extreme deviance: mass homicide. "School shooters often target those at the top of the social hierarchy, the jocks and the preps, at least in their initial hit lists, a pattern that supports the notion that the entire institution is under attack. School shooters are seeking to overturn – possibly destroy – the status system that has relegated them to the miserable bottom" (Newman et al., 2004: 248–9).

From this synthesis of the analysis of the best evidence available on rampage school shootings, we can see that the final extreme deviant action of mass murder by otherwise ordinary teenagers is the result of an interactive process among the various elements: individual biology, psychology, situation, relationships, institution, social structure, and culture. At all points in the process, interacting individuals are making strained and structured choices; in the case of the rampage school shooter, these choices become increasingly narrowed until they reach a perceived point of "no choice," which results in their violent act. It should be noted here that I am not saying that extreme acts of deviance, or any other acts of deviance for that matter, are explained by rational choice theory. Just because choices are involved as part of the process does not mean that choice is responsible for the outcome. Rather, choice about how to react to, or what to do about, the pain of suffering is one component of a complex, interactive, reciprocal set of social processes that take place over time. These processes, and the meanings that are socially constructed by the actors and audiences, ultimately reduce the perceived options to a "no choice" situation. Paradoxically, the perceived powerlessness of their lives can be resolved by their final exit explosion of rage, through which they can escape their pain, regardless of the consequences, since they will no longer be there to feel it.

Mundane deviance

While the interactive patterns of everyday deviant behavior don't result in the extremely disastrous outcomes seen in the rampage-shooting example, familiar patterns can be found in daily deviance. People's past experiences render some behaviors available to them as current choices, while closing off others which are not and have never been part of their behavioral scope. Their present biographical situation may encourage conventional behavior or oppose it, nudging a search for more unconventional options. Put simply, people may be more or less willing to deviate. They are rarely forcibly coerced into deviant action; but neither are they wholly free. Moreover, their present choices are not equal because their own past experiences have been unique. But they are patterned, since some social groups – particularly the physically, socially, or psychologically abused – have been subject to broadly similar conditions. Yet even within these categories, patterns of behavior are variable. I have used an extreme example above to illustrate the process of interactive decision making that can lead to extreme deviance, and it should not go unnoted that the initial rule-creators and enforcers constructed the marginalized category that ultimately brought about more violent deviance. This is not an uncommon outcome, especially if research on child abuse, sexual abuse, and physical abuse is reviewed. Other examples of "extreme deviance," as sociologist of deviance Erich Goode and D. Angus Vail (2007) have called it, include activities such as extreme tattooing, adult–child sexual contact (pedophilia), alien abductees, white supremacists, and sadomasochists and others who derive pleasure from their own or others' pain. However, most deviance, of the kind many of us engage in, is not of this extreme nature and involves far less dramatic or harmful outcomes; yet it is no less an interactive process involving the social construction of meaning.

In the mid-1970s, Alexander Liazos shook the field of deviance studies by accusing sociologists of focusing on the exceptional, bizarre, and dramatic behaviors of those who were often powerless, while ignoring other deviance that occurs in the rest of society, among so-called "normals." In particular, he thought that the term "deviance" itself tended to apologize for, and accommodate, deviance among the powerless. In the process, sociologists failed to study deviance among the powerful. He said: "As a result of the fascination with 'nuts, sluts, and perverts,' and their identities and subcultures, little attention has been paid to the unethical, illegal, and destructive actions of powerful individuals, groups, and institutions in our society" (Liazos, 1972: 26). What started as a study of difference, diversity, and the plight of the underdog evokes a sympathy and tolerance that masks deviance in regular institutions, particularly institutional violence. Examples of deviance by the powerful have since become a significant focus of both sociology and criminology, with books on corporate and white collar crime, banking fraud, and other forms of deviance by the powerful. Indeed David Simon's book *Elite Deviance* is currently in its ninth edition (Simon, 2008). Other notable contributors to this refocusing of the deviancy imagination are reflected in such titles as: *Banking on Fraud*, *Trusted Criminals*, *Profit without Honor* and *Corporate and Government Deviance*.

Between the extreme deviance discussed in the previous example and deviance by the powerful elites lies a whole range of ordinary deviant behavior that we call "mundane deviance." The term "mundane deviance" refers to rule-breaking that goes on every day but is relatively undramatic – in many cases, routine. As such, this kind of deviance fits into the field of study covered by the *Journal of Mundane Behavior*, established in 2000 to explore what sociologist Wayne Brekhus (2000) describes in his "Mundane Manifesto" as "analytically interesting studies of the socially uninteresting . . . an explicit social science of the unmarked (mundane)." He argues:

> The study of social life often neglects the ordinary in favor of the extraordinary. Historians study "eventful" time periods more than "uneventful" ones, cultural anthropologists are generally drawn to distant and exotic cultures rather than familiar ones, sociologists tend to study important social problems over quotidian reality, and journalists focus more on extraordinary individuals and groups than ordinary ones.

Brekus says that we "actively attend to and thus 'mark' some items of our social environment while ignoring, and thus leaving 'unmarked,' others" (2000). He says that signifying or marking some aspects of social life throws them into relief "as exceptional and *socially specialized*" (2000). In contrast, "the unmarked represents the vast expanse of social reality that is passively defined as unremarkable and *socially generic*" (Brekhus, 1998: 35). In his article "A Sociology of the Unmarked," Brekhus outlines five basic properties of "the markedness relationship":

> 1) the marked is heavily articulated while the unmarked remains unarticulated; 2) as a consequence, the marking process exaggerates the importance and distinctiveness of the marked; 3) the marked receives disproportionate attention relative to its size or frequency, while the unmarked is rarely attended to even though it is usually greater; 4) distinctions within the marked tend to be ignored, making it appear more homogeneous than the unmarked; and 5) characteristics of a marked member are generalized to all members of the marked category but never beyond the category, while attributes of an unmarked member are either perceived as idiosyncratic to the individual or universal to the human condition. (1998: 36)

As we have seen, these qualities are amplified and reproduced by studies of social deviance, particularly where these examine extreme deviance: "As a consequence, much social research inadvertently perpetuates rather than challenges stereotypical thinking" (Brekhus, 2000). Although Brekhus and the *Journal of Mundane Behavior* are specifically advocating that we analyze conformity, ironically conformity must also contain deviance since, as one reflective observer has noted from this perspective, "deviance is average": it is "startlingly normal (defined as commonly occurring and acceptable). Our days are filled with transgressions of varying magnitude, some our own and some those of others" (Nesbeth, 2008). So the kind of "deviance studied could be office workers or why the Japanese behave strangely in elevators according to Westerners," becoming uncharacteristically friendly because "the close quarters and fleeting duration of the ride encourage passengers to deviate from the rigid social scripts that govern Japanese cultural life" (Eakin, 2000). Indeed, sociologist Scott Schaffer says, "What has emerged is a concern with looking at how large social systems shape and are constituted by the social interactions we engage in daily" (quoted by Eakin, 2000). We will return to the centrality of the margins in the concluding chapter.

For most people, then, rule-breaking is episodic, neither totally conventional, nor completely deviant. Most people flirt with convention and conformity, postponing commitment and evading decision, a point first noted by sociologist David Matza among juvenile delinquents. To do otherwise would be to submit to the tyranny of structured roles and allow individuality and freedom to escape us. Indeed, for most of us, deviance is tied to particular situations and its practice is of short duration, though may be repeated. People are often rule-breakers but rarely are they fully deviants, if that is taken to mean that they systematically engage in repetitive and all-consuming anti-social behavior. How people maintain a commitment to convention while simultaneously breaking conventional rules is a crucial part of the process of becoming deviant. Indeed, if we are freed of any moral qualms about the acts that are part of our behavioral scope, then we are free, if not compelled, to commit them. The process whereby this comes about is called "neutralization." In the next chapter we'll examine how "neutralizations" and motives come together to further explain why people act deviantly.

4

Neutralizing morality and deviant motivations

In the previous chapter we argued that most social deviance is "normal" in the sense that it occurs in almost all social settings and, as a result, is "mundane." Studies on honesty and dishonesty, for example, reveal that 85 percent of the population is found to be less than completely honest, and those who are completely honest and totally trustworthy are statistically deviant – often to the point of being excluded from "in" groups because they make the regular, somewhat deviant, majority population feel uncomfortable.

However, being somewhat deviant does not make people excessively deviant or deeply deviant or extremely deviant. Most people are not committed to a deviant or delinquent lifestyle. If most people have a commitment at all, and that is questionable, it is to conventionality. If it were otherwise, we would need to transcend our culture, our parental influences, and our interpersonal connections; doing so, we would quickly become exhausted by the effort. Most people, most of the time, behave according to accepted norms. Here, commitment might best be described as partial, since beliefs and values in conventionality may be temporarily suspended by virtue of the meaning that is constructed about a particular situation or event. Words and phrases may gloss over a situation in such a way that a person is freed from any moral constraint that might otherwise be felt. In this chapter we will first explore these multiple ways that ordinary people excuse and justify their involvement in deviant behavior in such a way that the very words and phrases they use can form a "vocabulary of motives" that can result in deviant behavior. This is called "neutralization theory." The central idea behind neutralization theory is that "the excuses and justifications that deviants use to rational-ize their behaviors might themselves be implicated in the etiology of deviant behavior" (Maruna and Copes, 2004: 2). First, let's look at the way we use words and phrases in relation to questionable behavior. Later we will look at other motives involved in the decision to deviate.

Excuses, justification, and the timing of accounts

Excuses are words or phrases, known as "accounts," that people say in order to deny their responsibility for the acts that they accept are morally wrong; justifications are the accounts people give to accept responsibility for acts that they deny are morally wrong. Together, excuses and justi-fications can be given in answer to questioning others, after an act has been committed, in order to reject accusations of culpability for the consequences of the act. If the audience doing the questioning, or holding someone to account, "honors," respects, or accepts these explanations, the person acting deviantly may not suffer any severe consequences. However, such excuses or justificatory accounts given *after* the act in question are suspect since the account giver may be rationalizing the act in order to deny or reduce their culpability and the negative consequences of such "remedial work." The function of remedial work "is to alter the meaning that otherwise might be given to an act, transforming what could be seen as offensive into what could be seen as acceptable" (Goffman, 1971: 139). Whether this works depends upon what are seen as acceptable accounts.

If, instead, as criminologist Donald Cressey (1953) observed in his study of embezzlers, people contemplate the act in advance *before* engag-ing in it, and anticipate that they might be questioned after the fact, they might, in a Machiavellian way, role-play in conversations with them-selves to determine whether their account will be accepted or rejected. If, in these thought experiments, the potential deviant sees that the range of vocabularies available would lack credibility, not be believed or accepted, and if he or she, therefore, refrains from the activity because of the absence of a credible account, then the words or phrases can be seen as acting as a social control of that behavior.

In contrast, if the potential deviant does find credibility in the words and phrases that might be used in the face of moral questioning and decides to commit the act, these words will have acted as "vocabularies of motive," allowing the deviant behavior to proceed. Indeed, for embez-zlers, using words and phrases to convince themselves they are only "borrowing the money" and that they "intend to pay it back" can lead them to embezzle. As Cressey (1970: 111) said, after studying embezzlers' motives, "I am convinced that the words the potential embezzler uses in his conversation with himself are actually the most important elements in the process that gets him into trouble." Cressey calls this use of words and phrases, after contemplating the act but before committing it, "verbalizations."

Clearly then, the timing of words and phrases that we use in conversations with ourselves is important. So, what happens if the words and phrases are a part of the subculture or social environment that we inhabit, such as a work place or a peer group? That an environment can be awash with neutralizing words and phrases that make up our meaningful world, and that these become taken-for-granted background assumptions of our daily life, means that these contexts are themselves neutralizing. They are social contexts that remove any moral qualms prior to even contemplating an act. It is in this sense that David Matza argued people could "unwittingly" neutralize the moral bind of law. Doing so sends their user on a "moral holiday" from where they might contemplate acts of deviance, not because they are inherently deviant, but because the acts are desirable, available, and possible. Moreover, where the subculture sets the norms, societal deviance may become the norm for everyone in the group. In such circumstances, conventional or non-deviant behavior is deviant and is the behavior that has to be accounted for. Consider the case of college drinking, where there is pressure put on fellow students to party. Not partying is seen as deviant and needs explaining to fellow students in order to maintain social acceptance among the group. Accounts explaining commitments to schoolwork and girlfriends are acceptable exceptions allowing deviance from the norm of drinking. Simply doing nothing, but not drinking either, results in disapproval, and that disapproval becomes more intense the more often invitations to drinking parties are declined. The ultimate sanction is exclusion from friendship groups for those who persistently abstain.

Techniques of neutralization

The use of words and phrases to neutralize morality, either consciously or unconsciously, has been a major feature in explaining deviance since David Matza's early studies in 1957. Unfortunately, use of the term "technique" implies that these are only instruments in the sense of ulterior devices. However, it is clear from Matza's (1964) later work, and our previous discussion, that their timing is critical, as is whether or not these words and phrases are part of the meaningful environment or imported into that environment by design. Since Matza first introduced the original five techniques of neutralization, others have been documented, and in this section we will review ten types and illustrate how they are used.

(1) Denial of responsibility. Denial of responsibility is the classic excuse that claims that the offender is acting because of forces beyond his control, reflected in the phrase "it wasn't my fault." These morally neutralizing words may deny that one is responsible for a potentially deviant act, perhaps claiming that "under the circumstances I had no choice," or "I was not myself" because "I had one or two drinks." Consider the case of a college footballer, Troy, who had been taking steroids for thirteen months: "He began taking them because the coaching staff had changed his position on the team, so he needed to add as much strength and size as possible: 'They made me do it. I was too little and weak to play there'" (Clark, 1999: 84).

(2) Denial of injury. Denial of injury is a justification based on the claim that the action didn't cause others any harm and, since harm is the cultural reason for behavior to be offensive, then the behavior is not immoral. For example, restaurant staff steal and eat food and have been known to justify this on the basis that the restaurant is not losing because so much is wasted anyway that their food consumption makes no difference: "I feel we should be charged for entrée items, but stuff like bread sticks, soup, salad, and desserts should be free. After all, customers receive these items in unlimited quantity, and half the time they waste most of it" (Stafford, 1999: 52–3). Hospital employees who pilfer might claim that the hospital doesn't lose: "the hospital won't miss it and I'm sure that whatever they find missing they can write off on their taxes or as a donation or something" (Fairchild, 1999: 63).

(3) Denial of victim. Denial of victim is a justification. It does not claim that there is no victim (that is denial of injury). Rather the claim is that the person "offended" doesn't have the right to claim victim status because they were the original offender and deserved what happened to them as retribution, to balance or restore justice. Thus, denial of victim questions the right of the supposed victim to moral sanctuary on the grounds that "he asked for it," or "they had it coming," or it was "only retaliation for them hurting me." The example of restaurant scams provides an illustration:

> Waitress Jo . . . told me she didn't always ask [the cooks] for free food but when she did, it was usually after an extremely slow or busy shift. She justified this by the fact that during slow times she didn't make

any money in tips and the hourly rate was ridiculously low, proving to herself that "the restaurant owes me this." She used the same justification after working a busy shift in which she was unable take a break or was forced to deal with an unusual amount of stress during her shift. (Lockhart, 1999: 56)

A similar example is found with hospital employee, "Jack," who is a chronic pilferer: "I've taken batteries, rubber bands, staples, and the stapler, pencils and pens . . . garbage bags, plastic buckets, bed sheets and pillowcases." Jack says he hates his job, hates his supervisor, and argues that the hospital doesn't pay him enough. He says what he takes is "a shift differential" to make up for what he doesn't get (Fairchild, 1999: 63). Bad supervisors are often cited as a reason for employee deviance. Jack continues:

I don't like her and I can take or leave the job. But I've no choice. She comes with the job. But she really never listens to our needs. She never knows what's going on in the lab until it's too late. Then when her supervisors start to shit on her, she shits on us. I don't like the job because there is no room for progress . . . I feel that the way this place treats you, you should be entitled to whatever you want. The verbal and mental abuse they put you through is too much. A paycheck isn't enough to compensate for the stress you're under. (Fairchild, 1999: 63–4)

Or, in the words of a shopping mall security officer who has a variety of schemes to earn extra money or perks on the job, talking about his follow officers:

they believe the company "shafts" them in many ways and that by taking things from the company they get even . . . I guess there is something of a revenge motive there. In the eyes of most officers they are only taking what they worked for. The wages in this kind of work are so low that they see this as a way of making up the difference. (Malone, 1999: 68)

Importantly, denial of the victim is precisely the neutralization that underlies the accounts of the rampage school shooters discussed earlier. They believed that the years of abuse they had suffered justified their retaliation. Consider the example of school shooter Luke Woodham, who said: "I killed because people like me are mistreated everyday . . . I suffered all my life . . . I was ridiculed, always beaten, always hated . . . I have a right to be angry, society treated me like dirt" (cited by Newman et al., 2004: 249–50). This neutralization allows the sense of "righteous slaughter" that these victims of abuse felt, which also explains their common lack of remorse.

(4) Condemnation of the condemners. Condemning the condemners justifies questioned behavior by challenging the right of others, particularly officials in society who judge, to make judgments, because they too are engaged in similar or worse behavior. This use of morally neutralizing words and phrases challenges the moral superiority of those asking condemning questions by, for example, pointing to Catholic priests who are practicing pedophiles, police being corrupt, senior government officials lying to elected legislators, and elected politicians selling political offices (even Senate seats!) for personal profit. In the restaurant example, when pointing out that the failure to pay for her own meal was theft, the waitress justified this by saying she had witnessed the same kind of behavior from management.

(5) Appeal to higher loyalties. Appeal to higher loyalties justifies a questioned behavior based on the claim that the offender was following higher moral values than those of the people judging. To the potential deviant, their immediate group, such as "homeboys," "bros," may be so important that wider and more abstract loyalties are lost to the moment, as in: "I was only helping my mates." For example, in a study of "snitching" on fellow naval midshipmen, sociologist Jana Pershing (2003) found that failure to report violations of the rules to higher officers in the Navy was justified by the loyalty and peer friendships among these close-knit groups. This is similar to the observations about the use of performance-enhancing drugs by college football players: "Non-using team players provided a protective shield of conspiratorial silence for their using colleagues. They condemned them only if publicity, through being caught, brought condemnation on the team; but otherwise they saw drug use as an individual decision that enhanced the overall team performance" (Henry and Eaton, 1999: 77–8). Alternatively, wider loyalties than those of secular humanity, such as "it was God's will" may supplant the general morality of the situation. Our steroid-using college football player, Troy, justified his drug use stating: "I know it's not right, but hell I wanted to play. It's for the love of the game" (Clark, 1999: 84). Indeed, the justification given for the continued practice of buying alcohol for under-age college fraternity members, regardless of the laws against this, are loyalty to those fraternity traditions and to the membership of the fraternity, over the requirements of the university rules or the law.

(6) Metaphor of the ledger. "Metaphor of the ledger" refers to those words and phrases through which the person accepts that the act in

question was wrong but asks the questioners to place the act in a wider context of all the behavior committed over his life; to take account of the whole character of the person, the good and the bad, with the claim that, on balance, the person is good, as in the classic case of Carl Klockars' (1973) *Professional Fence*, "Vincent Swaggi," who talked about the money he'd given to charity and help he'd given to children: "Sure I've done some bad things, but if you add up all the good things and weigh them against the bad things, I've got to come out on the good side." This is similar to the cyber-porn surfer and well-respected church member, interviewed by Tyrone Good, who explained that "his good deeds in the church youth group far exceed the amount of time and energy he spends seeking prospective sex partners in Internet chat rooms" (Good, 1999: 43).

A variation of this type of neutralization is to accept that the behavior is immoral but to argue that the circumstances justify it, and to claim that their future persona and behavior will be different; that this is only a phase of their life and not their real self. Consider this account of a stripper who is a single parent and a student: " 'I plan to leave this place and them [clients] as soon as I graduate. Their money allows me to be both a good student and a mom. As soon as I can support my family on a normal job's pay, I am so outta this crazy life' " (Turner, 1999: 34). Turner comments: "She claims the label 'tramp' that others see her as 'will not always be her' " (1999: 34).

(7) Claim of normality. The claim of normality challenges the idea of statistical deviance, arguing, as in Gabor's (1994) book *Everyone's Doing It!*, that "everybody cheats on their taxes and embezzles from their employer." The claim then is that the questioned behavior is normal rather than deviant, with the implication that its moral or deviant status should not be questioned. Consider college football player Earl's comment on his use of Creatine, a bodybuilding supplement: "Everybody in this game is looking for a way to better himself. That's what I did" (Clark, 1999: 85); or college fraternity members buying alcohol for minors: "Everyone else in every other fraternity in this country is doing the exact same thing" (Bradley, 1999: 95); or restaurant staff who claim that everybody steals from their employer.

(8) Denial of negative intent. Denial of negative intent uses words and phrases that accept responsibility for any harm caused by the act but claim that the offender did not intend the negative outcome because they were "just having fun," or that it was "just a joke," as in the student firing bottle rockets at fellow students from his campus dorm room: "If people want to disapprove of my behavior I don't care...I feel I

shouldn't have to be confronted by their opinion . . . if they can't take a joke, then to hell with them" (Moss, 1999: 136).

(9) Claim of relative acceptability. The claim of relative acceptability places the questioned behavior in the context of other deviant behavior that is more serious, arguing that, relatively, it is acceptable by being less harmful or less serious. For example, people who date members of the opposite sex outside of their marriage have said: "I'm not sleeping with these people. Females as well as males can have friends of the opposite sex without any type of sexual involvement"; "Having a friend is not cheating. Having a friend and sleeping with him is cheating" (Frost, 1999: 31). Citing worse behavior makes the actual behavior relatively acceptable. The same use of moral distinctions has been made by naval officers who cheat on their spouses, in which cheating while deployed overseas is seen as relatively acceptable, compared to cheating while at home, and having sex "on the spur of the moment isn't as bad as premeditated" (Shea, 2007: 59). So too with pilfering military equipment among soldiers in the Army:

> Equipment was seen as one of three types: "personal property," "unit property" and "equipment that you find." There seemed to be strong informal rules against taking personal equipment: "You never take someone else's stuff because they would have to pay for it." A person who gets caught taking personal gear is looked down upon by everyone in the unit. He is seen as a despicable person and not to be trusted. In contrast soldiers generally felt that it was alright to take the unit's property . . . As one soldier said "it belongs to the Army and they're always wasting money so who cares. . . . Nor was anything seen as wrong with taking equipment that was found . . . Since the lost item didn't really belong to anyone it was alright to take it home." (North, 1999: 69)

Finally, consider the case of athletes taking steroids to become more competitive: "Those who use steroids do not see themselves as drug takers in the way that narcotics users are seen as drug addicts. They feel that unlike narcotics, steroids are not detrimental to society even though both are illegal. Steroids produce an overall positive effect on the body, whereas narcotics produce a negative effect on the mind and body . . . Steroids build up the body not break it down" (Michaels, 1999: 81).

(10) Claim of privilege to deviate. The claim of privilege to deviate (or deviance as deserved rewards) is the justification that, because of a major investment of energy, risk, or courage, the person deserves "deviant

rewards" as compensation and should be indulged because of their supreme sacrifice. In her study of naval deployment and adultery, Jennifer Shea (2007: 60–1) found that some deployed naval officers saw cheating on their spouses as a reward "for hard work and . . . for service to your country, so you deserve a break and to have some fun . . . When you are deployed you have a sense of entitlement because you're away from home and fighting for your country, so it helps to rationalize it."

These ten categories of neutralization are indicative of those that have been found. Indeed, in a major review of the field entitled "Excuses, Excuses: What Have We Learned from Five Decades of Neutralization Research?" criminologists Shadd Maruna and Heath Copes argue that not only are the original five techniques of neutralization not necessarily the most important techniques, and are anyway somewhat overlapping (e.g. denial of injury and denial of victim), but also "researchers have identified dozens (even hundreds, depending how finely one cuts them) of techniques that seem to serve the same function as neutralization techniques. What is interesting about neutralization theory is this function (what the neutralizations do), not the flavors it comes in" (Maruna and Copes, 2004: 64). Neutralization, then, involves the use of words and phrases in ways that make people feel it is morally acceptable to engage in deviant behavior. Neutralization makes deviance a non-moral issue. A fundamental question concerns the timing of their use. Most studies of deviance have been done on those who participate after the fact, so it is difficult to know whether these morally freeing words and phrases were in place prior to the act or were invoked as after-the-fact rationalizations. Others question why some people find the need to use morally neutralizing words and phrases to excuse or justify their behavior and others do not. The fact remains that, for those who neutralize their commitment to convention through neutralization, the only remaining issue is one of motive.

Motives for deviance

The intriguing question that most people ask when they think of others' deviant behavior is: what motivates them to do it? Motives are the attractions, rewards, or satisfactions that propel us to action. It is imagined that, because the behavior we see as deviance in others is so different from anything we ourselves may do, it requires some special kind of motivation. However, as we have seen, what it requires is that any moral question be suspended or at least rendered unclear or ambiguous, or for it not to exist in the first place. Once morality is a non-issue, then the question of "why do they do it?" becomes easier to answer. In fact, most deviance is motivated by exactly the same set of motives as non-deviant behavior. The range of motives is vast but can be clustered into five main categories, although some of these are overlapping – such as fun, excitement, and sex:

(a) Pecuniary, material or tangible motives: to make money, to obtain goods or services, to obtain sex.
(b) Recreational motives: to enjoy fun and excitement, to obtain thrills, to play; to get high; to beat the system (seen as a game).
(c) Interpersonal or social motives: to achieve status; to earn honor and prestige; to repay favors; to gain acceptance, fit in or feel normal; to stand out; to express friendship, loyalty or resentment; to fulfill role expectations; to compete or meet a challenge.
(d) Problem-solving motives: to relieve pain, stress, tension or boredom; to establish identity; to compensate for missing expectations; to cope; to avoid or escape responsibility; to preserve self (self-defense); to restore control over one's life.
(e) Political motives: to correct injustices; to gain domination over others; to gain freedom from others; to beat an oppressive system; to change society or parts of a social system; to express allegiance to alternative religious, moral or ethical beliefs.

(Henry and Eaton, 1999: 20–1)

This is not an exhaustive list but indicative of the range of possibilities. It is clear that, for any particular act of deviance, several of these motives may be in effect simultaneously, yet others may be not present at all. Consider, for example, the case of rampage school shooters. Their motives are a combination of: resentment; relief and escape from pain, stress, and tension; to preserve a sense of self (albeit resulting in their own destruction); to momentarily restore control over their lives (while ultimately giving up that control); to correct injustices; to gain freedom from others' control over them; to change parts of the social system (the peer subcultures of the school); and in some cases to gain prestige and stand out as (in)famous. The same kind of analysis can be conducted with different kinds of deviance, recognizing that all who engage in any particular behavior do not do it for the same motives, but also display a range of motives. Our student studies in deviant behavior are illustrative. For example, some of Good's (1999: 43) cyber-porn surfers were clearly engaged in their deviance for the thrill of deviant sex, seeing those who don't engage "as robots who were either afraid or not versatile enough to engage in the behaviors that they found to be second nature." But others were expressing liberation politics or ethical motives, such as a "dominant mistress" who said she was "only exercising her true right as a woman to exceed the sexual limitations placed on her by a 'closed-minded' society." Further, she influenced her daughter to engage in the same behavior, so that "when she gets of age she will be free of the restrictions that a patriarchal society places on her" (1999: 44).

Jill Turner's (1999) observations in a high-class topless dancing establishment reveal deviant practices such as giving clients personal attention and sex. While sex and entertainment services may be the motives for their clients, their own motives involve power, control, and money, which the dancers say frees them from the control of others:

> As a recent divorcee and single parent, now having her own income, Morgan feels free from her ex-husband's demands or threats of holding back child support. The freedom and control provided by stripping echoes the finding by others who see stripping and dating customers as providing power and control for women who feel out of control or who are controlled by others. (1999: 34)

At the same time, some strippers get a sense of fulfillment from helping others. For example, after going on a dinner date with a paying male client who claimed he needed someone to talk with about his wife's menopause, stripper Tiffany asked Jill, who accompanied them on the date, " 'Don't you feel good? We actually helped that guy and his marriage. There are worse things we could do for money.' Tiffany admits though not all of her dates are of the talking kind. She has convinced herself that the service she provides helps other people, doesn't hurt anyone and gives her economic stability" (1999: 35). (Note also the claims of relative acceptability and denial of injury here.) In contrast, as we saw at the outset of this chapter, in the low-class strip club, Shaw (1999: 39–40) found that money and drugs were the major motives, as was the often-felt need to escape from abusive relationships.

Examples of drug and alcohol use may at first seem to be tied up with motives of thrill seeking, having fun and excitement. However, Page's (1999) account of tailgate or parking lot parties demonstrates that loyalty to an intimate group can be a motive for student alcohol use:

> the consumption of alcohol actually provides the medium around which intimate social groups could meet in a public setting. In this case alcohol changes an otherwise neutral setting to one in which boredom and loneliness can be relieved. Interestingly, alcohol is the catalyst and the subsequent group interaction and trust provides the motive for continued meeting. The group founded on drinking became a substitute family for those who, for a variety of reasons, had become isolated from other groups and contacts. (Henry and Eaton, 1999: 91–2)

The drinking group also served as an alternative way to meet friends without having to join circles in which drug use had become a norm (Page, 1999). Less obvious motives for college drinking than the typical fun, release of tension, and relaxation of inhibitions also appear in Bradley's (1999) account of fraternity drinking: "These include the pride from having a reputation of being able to drink more than others or for being able to purchase alcohol for minors . . . a return of favors to a system that provided such services to the purchaser when they were also underage." Other observations on student drinking behavior show that it is accompanied by peer pressure and stigmatization concerning the frequency of drinking, and the amount one is supposed to drink, with social sanctioning and pressure being put on those who don't fit in.

Failure to commit to conformity

So far we have examined cases where people who otherwise behave conventionally have seen their morality suspended or eroded, allowing them to be free to act depending upon what motivates them. Of course, people may also deviate because they have no particular commitment to conformity. If bonding relations are absent and no attachments have been formed with conventional parents and other supposedly conventional actors, such as schools, churches, or community groups, or if there is no stake in the conventional society, little involvement in its institutions, or a low level of belief in its norms and values, then deviance is likely to be an available choice. More accurately, we might say that convention is not particularly attractive if there is nothing in it for those in need of pleasure, and, further, it is not attractive if there is nothing in it to lose. Sociologist Travis Hirschi, who referred to it as control theory, developed this explanation for deviance – in particular, delinquency by youth; absence of controls meant a person was more likely to commit deviant or delinquent acts:

Hirschi identified four levels of the failure to develop this stake in convention: (1) "attachment," (2) "commitment," (3) "involvement," and (4) "belief." Attachment is the caring and sensitivity a person has for conventional others' feelings, opinions, and well-being; conventional others include parents, teachers, religious leaders, members of the community. Strong bonds of attachment would mean acting in a way that respects those conventional others, taking care not to hurt them. Commitment is the fear that one needs to preserve a relationship with conventional actors and avoid losing one's stake or investment in the relationship. Involvement suggests that the more conventional activity – such as school-related activity, clubs and societies, community volunteer work, etc. – that one engages in, the less time there is for deviant activity; conversely, those less involved in convention have more free time in which to deviate, as in "the Devil makes work for idle hands." Finally, there is the view that it is important to believe in conventional values, to follow conventional rules, and to uphold conventional morality: "delinquency is not caused by beliefs that require delinquency, but is rather made possible by the absence of (effective) beliefs that forbid delinquency" (Hirschi, 1969: 26). By way of illustration of the operation of social bonding to convention and how it functions to prevent deviance:

> let us consider the example of two college seniors, Trevor and Shantell, who have fallen in love, feel like soul mates, spend a lot of time together, respect each other, and plan to get married upon graduation. In a new criminology class, Trevor meets an attractive sophomore, Donna, who "just wants to have fun." The opportunity arises for a date during which Trevor would be tempted to cheat on his longtime girlfriend, Shantell. How do Hirschi's key concepts explain what might unfold? Strong attachment means that Trevor would not go on the date, because he knows it would be disrespectful toward Shantell, who would feel upset and betrayed. Strong commitment means that Trevor has led Shantell to trust in him. Such a date, especially given whom it was with, would be cheating on his relationship. This would undermine the trust between Trevor and Shantell and risk the breakup of the relationship and cancellation of their planned marriage. Strong involvement in the relationship with Shantell would mean that Trevor was so busy doing activities with her that there literally would not be time for anyone else. Finally, strong belief in their relationship would include reference to certain values such as honesty, safety, monogamy, stability, security, and maybe even the belief that taking risks is unwise. In short, Hirschi's bonded conventional student, Trevor, would probably reject the date, recognizing that it threatened his valued relationship with Shantell. Of course, if he justified the act to himself with the arguments that the date with Donna would be a onetime kind of thing, that his steady would not know about it, and she would be working anyway, he would not be a Hirschi-bonded student, but a Matza-neutralizing drifter off on a moral holiday, free to date Donna, at least on this occasion! (Lanier and Henry, 2004: 185)

Related to social bonding to convention is the effectiveness of socialization into convention, and in particular the idea of self-control. It has been a long tradition in thinking about social deviance to point to the numerous ways that socialization fails to produce social conformity. The basic assumption is that, unless socialized into conventional behavior, humans are capable of a wide range of behavior, including deviant behavior: "All of us, it appears, are born with the ability to use force and fraud in pursuit of our private goals." Moreover, "everyone is capable of criminal or deviant acts . . . however . . . some are more likely than others to actually commit them" (Hirschi and Gottfredson, 2001: 88). Humans are all born with impulses and motives to deviate and this is a normal, not a pathological, state; in order to limit or control those impulses we have to be effectively socialized to repress or control them. Socialization is typically seen as the ways in which first parents, and then schools, inculcate children with respect for the values and norms of conventional society. This is achieved through monitoring the children's behavior, recognizing when it is inappropriate, correcting it when it deviates, and providing a structure or framework through which to act appropriately, with due consideration for others:

> But the major sources of self-control, in our view, are the actions of parents or other responsible adults. Parents, who care for their children, watch them as best they can. When they see their children doing something they should not do, they correct, admonish, or punish them. The logical structure of successful socialization thus has four necessary conditions: care, monitor, recognize (deviant behavior) and correct. When all of these conditions are present, the child presumably learns to avoid acts with long-term negative consequences, whatever their legal or moral status. When any one of them is missing, continued low self-control may be the result. (2001: 90)

Indeed, Hirschi and Gottfredson argue: "By the age of 8 or 10, most of us learn to control such tendencies to the degree necessary to get along at home and at school . . . low self-control is natural and . . . *self-control is acquired* in the early years of life. Children presumably learn from many sources to consider the long-range consequences of their acts" (2001: 90). Particularly important as reinforcement for learning self-control beyond the family is the school:

> First it can more effectively monitor behavior than the family, with one teacher overseeing many children at a time. Second, as compared to most parents, teachers generally have no difficulty recognizing deviant or disruptive behavior. Third, as compared to the family, the school has such a clear interest in maintaining order and discipline that it can be expected to do what it can to control disruptive behavior. Finally, like the family, the school in theory has the authority and means to punish lapses in self-control. (Gottfredson and Hirschi, 1990: 105)

If effective child rearing occurs through family and school, then high levels of self-control will be established and the probability of deviance will be minimized. In contrast, if ineffective child socialization occurs, low levels of self-control will be manifest as impulsivity, insensitivity, risk-taking behavior; low-self-control individuals act to obtain immediate gratification, demonstrating little understanding of deferred gratification or long-term future planning. Such people are much more likely to participate in social deviance and to continue to do so over their life course:

> Those who have a high degree of self-control avoid acts potentially damaging to their future prospects, whatever current benefits these acts seem to promise. Those with a low degree of self-control are easily swayed by current benefits and tend to forget future costs. Most people are between these extremes, sometimes doing things they know they should not do, other times being careful not to take the unnecessary risks for short-term advantage. (Hirschi and Gottfredson, 2001: 82)

In self-control theory, a major distinction is made between the acts of crime and the potential for committing such acts, i.e. a person's criminality: "the tendency of people to engage in or refrain from criminal acts" (2001: 88). So, it is in this view assumed that everyone is capable of criminal or deviant acts, and that "some are more likely than others to actually commit them. Criminality is a matter of degree" (2001: 88). Thus the difference between those with the potential for committing acts of crime or deviance who don't and those with the potential who do is:

> in their awareness of and concern for the long-term costs of crime – such things as arrest, prison, disgrace, disease, and even eternal damnation . . . What distinguishes offenders from others is not the strength of their appetites but their freedom to enjoy the quick and easy and ordinary pleasures of crime without undue concern for the pains that may follow them . . . we thus infer the nature of criminality. People who engage in crime are people who neglect long-term consequences. They are, or tend to be, children of the moment. They have what we call low self-control. (2001: 90)

Persons with low self-control are considered to be insensitive to the feelings of others and lack empathy for suffering victims (Gottfredson and Hirschi, 1990: 88).

A simple rational-choice model of human nature is implied here, as Gottfredson and Hirschi (1990: 5) state:

> all human conduct can be understood as self-interested pursuit of pleasure or the avoidance of pain . . . It tells us that people behave rationally when they commit crimes and when they do not. It tells us that people are free to choose their course of conduct, whether it be

legal or illegal. And it tells us that people think of and act first for themselves, that they are not naturally inclined to subordinate their interests to the interests of others.

However, this idea of humans as effectively rational-choice thinkers applies less readily to those who abandon conventional values and the means to achieve them, and who slide into deviance as detachment from the apparent reality of a world to which they are unable to relate. Nor does it explain much of that which is irrational, such as the pursuit of pain and the avoidance of pleasure that characterizes some deviant behavior. Consider the case of those who self-mutilate to relieve their inner torment. Nor does it fully account for those who are highly bonded to conventional lives and institutions and yet deviate regardless, such as dentists abusing cocaine, doctors defrauding Medicare, and corporate executives embezzling from their companies. However, the rational-choice/interest model *is* an excellent way to understand why corporations defraud the public and employ risk managers to maximize their opportunities to do so while avoiding costs.

Clearly one of the main reasons why people may not have developed a commitment to conventional values is that they have developed a commitment to other values. This need not be because they lack self-control but simply because having examined, explored, thought about, and practiced conventional values, they find that these conventional values are meaningless, or boring. In their exploration for alternatives, they may have simply inverted the values of conventional society, alleviating their frustrated status position by constructing an alternative, oppositional, if rather defeatist, subculture. Alternatively, they might have inherited a subcultural commitment to alternative values either unwittingly, as a result of immersion in a culture that is outside the mainstream of society, or as a result of being in a culture subordinate to the mainstream, or by creating a culture that is designed to replace the mainstream. Then there are those who violate rules in order to further certain causes, and those who deviate in an attempt to advance the interests of their own deviant identities, refusing to accept negative judgments about what they do. Their deviance is certainly rational, but rarely impulsive; rather, it is often measured, calculated, and political.

Human biographies and meaningful contexts

To be shaped by one's background or to be shaped by the force of structural circumstance is to be in a context of past meanings from which newly created meaning is hewn. Values of convention or values of alternatives are the cloth from which new suits of deviant behavior are cut. Combining the meanings we have internalized from our socio-cultural environment with our personal experiences of what events and objects mean is necessary material for shaping the situation we are in at the present. But it also projects likely future courses of action; it suggests that we will have an affinity to some activities and an aversion to others. Even so, we are not completely compelled to act. We can choose, albeit under restricted, often narrowed and channeled conditions. The choice we make is unlikely to be something completely alien to our experience.

At most, we come to the decision to commit an act of deviance with more or less openness, more or less willingness, and more or less affinity or aversion. We are free to make choices in this context, but we are neither certain nor compelled to act in a particular way. What tips the balance of our choice and leads us to the initial decision to take part in the deviant act may depend quite literally on how open and willing we already are, taking account of the web of relations that we are in. It may equally depend on how we see the act furthering our self-identity, or how it adds to what we already see ourselves as being, not that this has to be decided urgently or impulsively. Alternatively, our reluctance to commit the act may be slowly worn away by the persistent requests of those with whom we are in friendly relations. As well as providing models that can be trusted, friends may also supply sufficient justification, role performance, materials, and skills to turn the next time they invite us to join with them into our first participation. These friends may finally tip the balance to provide our personal biographies with an excess of definitions favorable to rule violation. But it is important to recognize that it is still us who chooses. The difference is that, at this point in the process, our circumstances, our friends, our wider socio-cultural heritage, and our personal biographical experiences, including our family and socialization, have narrowed the possibilities from what was once merely one behavior in a vast array of others to an either/or issue.

The decision to try the behavior, at least once, may come as a great release. It certainly changes the whole situation. No longer are we solely dependent on our past meanings or those communicated to us through the words and actions of participating friends. We have now created space for further decisions based on our own experience, while simultaneously making available a repeat deviant performance on a future date. If our experience of the deviant activity was bad, we may have been turned off by the behavior. Having satisfied ourselves and our persuaders that we know what this deviance is, and do not like it personally, we may be unwilling to try it again. We are susceptible to the audience's translating the meaning of the activity from bad to neutral. But from neutral we may be prepared to try again, and once more, just to see if something was missed. We may continue to experiment. Repeated unfavorable experiences with a particular kind of deviance are likely to leave us in conformity or even with a renewed commitment to conformity. However, the experience may be sufficiently neutral or attractive that we are more willing to try the activity, if only to intensify it or simply because we have done it before and nothing particularly unpleasant happened. After a succession of increasingly favorable experiences, we may be prepared not merely to try the behavior one more time, but to actively seek it out as it increasingly becomes part of our biography. One may say that we are now "turned on" to the activity.

In this chapter, then, we have explored the range of factors that lead one to be more or less ready and morally free to commit deviant acts, and the variety of motivations that can make a deviant outcome more rather than less likely. In the next chapter, we go beyond how people arrive at the decision to experiment with deviant behavior and look at how people acquire or are conferred with "deviant" statuses.

5

How people become deviants

Robbie was born ... a normal, healthy baby, but during his fragile first months ... he got wired to violence as his parents' marriage devolved into a cage fight. "Mom and Dad were on the floor slugging it out," Molly [his mom] recalls. Before long, Rob's childhood became even more traumatic; several doctors would later conclude that at some point during these first years, Rob was molested ... [B]y the time he was four years old, Rob had grown into an attack machine. He was a menace on the playground, punching other kids and kicking them when he got upset. When teachers disciplined him he bit their hands ... Ronald [Robbie's father] brought his four-year-old son to the Methodist Richard Young Hospital and asked the psychiatrists what to do with the violent boy. The doctors asked Robbie why he kept hurting other kids. He lowered his eyes to the floor; "Because I'm stupid and bad," he mumbled. Committed to the hospital for observation, Rob behaved erratically ... He was diagnosed with depression and post-traumatic stress disorder ... caused by his hellish family life. After a month of heavy medication, the doctors sent him home with a warning that his recovery depended on continued therapy, and more important, having a stable, nurturing family environment. But stability was not his fate. Robbie returned to a chaotic custody battle between his parents, who were now divorced ... that culminated in Molly being dragged away in handcuffs and threatening Ronald's new wife Candice. Molly herself had quickly remarried ... and she was anxious to start a new family ... So after Candice had repeatedly called the police on Molly with charges of child endangerment, Molly gave up and surrendered her visitation rights to Rob ... She called her son into her room to explain the situation. By then Rob had been on regular doses of Thiordazine, the anti-psychotic drug, and Ritalin to treat attention deficit disorder . . . When Molly's abandonment finally sunk in, Rob turned his formidable anger against his step mother, Candice, the only maternal figure in his life, transferring onto her all the rage he must have felt toward his biological mother . . . Rob's father preferred to handle his outbursts by pinning him on the floor, sometimes for longer than an hour, until he would calm down. But when it was her turn to control him, Candice, an Air Force Vet, used the back of her hand. Growing up on a steady diet of psychiatric medication and corporal punishment, Rob became more violent and withdrawn. When he was 13, his ongoing battle with Candice went nuclear . . . For his 14th birthday Rob got another hospital admission and another fistful of pills . . . By now he no longer regretted his outbursts . . . not long after his father drove to juvenile court and asked the judge to take over . . . and the State Department of Health and Human Services became Rob's legal guardian . . . At 16 Rob was now a veteran of institutions, having spent the last 24 months in group homes because he resisted the reconciliation with Candice that would have allowed him to rejoin the family. He looked the part of a miserable ward of the state: painfully thin from years of under-eating, nails chewed to gnarled stubs. He wore his hair long, in a thick curtain that hid much of his face and obscured his eyes. He had been molested by another resident, and was prone to suicidal despair. In some ways he was even more traumatized than when he'd entered the system. . . . Over the years he kept trying to buck the rules and talk to his biological mother, with whom he held out hopes of a reunion, but he was never allowed to call her. By now his psychological profile included the darker, more exotic ailment that would lie behind his future crimes: anti-social personality disorder, a condition that makes it difficult, if not impossible to feel empathy for strangers. It is the underlying pathology of most serial killers. (Boal, 2008: 74–6)

In December 2007 Robert Hawkins, aged 18 shot and killed eight people at random with an AK-47 assault rifle while they were Christmas shopping at the Westroads Shopping Mall in Omaha, Nebraska, before killing himself. Robbie's situation is a clear example of the escalating effects that unstable and violent family life can have on the development of a person's identity, which culminates in a sense of worthlessness. In a suicide note prior to his mall massacre, he wrote: "I've been a piece of shit my entire life . . . It seems this is my only option" (2008: 80).

This chapter moves us from a person's willingness to engage in social deviance, to deviance as an inherent part of their social identity. Deviant behavior alone does not make a deviant. Nor does the repetition of that behavior make a deviant identity. According to sociologist Edwin Lemert, such episodic or repeated minor rule-breaking activity is no more than primary deviance because it is only a part of the range of available behavior: primary deviance is "polygenic, arising out of a variety of social, cultural, psychological, and physical factors . . . It has only marginal implications for the status and psychic structure of the person concerned" (Lemert, 1967: 40). At this stage in the deviance process there is no commitment, no identity doubt, and no identity transformation. Any guilt might be neutralized by the discourse of the context or by the application of learned techniques of neutralization. The rule-breaker is simply a person breaking rules, no more, no less.

In conversations with themselves, actors see their own essential being as non-deviant and their deviant behavior as incidental, occasional, or not their real selves. These are often deviant behaviors in the realm of exploration or experimentation. Sociologist Ross Matsueda observes that primary deviance "has only minor consequences for a person's status, social relationships, or subsequent behavior. Primary deviance tends to be situational transient and idiosyncratic" (Matsueda, 2001: 225). Initial participation in deviant behavior may result in repeat performances. But it does not result in an identity change. Experimenting with marijuana once, twice, or three times does not make a person "a stoner." Primary deviants will likely move on to other behaviors, do not become locked in a particular pattern of behavior, and see themselves as separate from the identity attributed to those labeled as "deviant." Thus, an occasional drug user is not a junkie; a social drinker is not an alcoholic; an exotic dancer, who occasionally dates her customer, is not a slut.

However, to produce the more serious, and arguably less escapable, secondary deviance, it is necessary for the person publicly identified as deviant to be excluded from normal activities, and that, in the process, they undergo a transformation of their self-identity. Only when an actor plays out a deviant activity as part of his/her identity, when s/he sees it as inevitable rather than selected, when his or her "life and identity are organized around the facts of deviance" (Lemert, 1967: 41) is that person referred to as a "secondary deviant." Secondary deviance, then, "is explicitly a response to societal reactions to deviance and has major consequences for a person's status, relationships and future behavior. Secondary deviance occurs when society's response to initial deviance (e.g. stigmatization, punishment, segregation) causes fundamental changes in the person's social roles, self-identity, and personality, resulting in additional deviant acts" (Matsueda, 2001: 225). The question addressed in this chapter is: how does deviant behavior get converted into deviant identity? Such conversion involves a repeated pattern of negative social reaction, moral judgment, degradation, and the recon-struction of past biography over time. It involves the action of audiences, whether these are other children, parents, teachers, counselors, mental health workers, courts, group homes, or correctional institutions – all of whom contribute to a social process of stigmatization and discrimina-tion. This process can begin early in life.

Psychologist John Bowlby (1988) emphasized the importance of having a secure emotional base in order to produce a developed personal-ity. He argued that children develop anxiety and insecurity if their par-enting is disrupted in their early years. This can occur as a result of experiencing traumatic events such as parental drug use or alcohol abuse, or child sexual abuse, or childhood abandonment because of separation from maternal bonding through placement in foster care or institutional care. As a result, these children, such as Robbie in our opening example, often have difficulty forming relationships. Such children lack the ability to empathize with others, becoming "affectionless children."

Clearly, the strength with which the others' views – i.e. the social self – are held, communicated, and imposed can affect a person's overall sense of self and this can build over time in a negative direction. This is especially important where others powerfully define one's status as deviant. Two fundamental concepts in understanding how one becomes a deviant are self-identity and the social self.

Self-identity, social self, and becoming deviant

Social psychologists have long recognized that people's self-identity is comprised of at least two interactive cognitive social processes. In one, we think of our unique and individual selves based upon our own biog-raphy; this is the person who we believe we are "deep down"; the true self, or the inner "I," such that, if there was no one else in the world to reflect back on us, this is who we would be. But since there are many others in the world and we interact with them in multiple ways in dif-ferent contexts, our identity is affected by their views. We are daily receiving communications, feedback, and clues about ourselves from what they tell us. What we make of what they tell us is critical for how we see ourselves, and who we become. We also have the ability to stand outside our inner selves and look at ourselves through others' eyes; we see ourselves as others see us. As Charles Horton Cooley (1902: 184) noted, this is "the imagination of our appearance to the other person; the imagination of his judgment of that appearance, and some sort of self-feeling such as mortification or pride." For social psychologist George Herbert Mead, the process involved taking the role of the other.

We take their role and try to look at ourselves as an object through another's eyes. Moreover, we can also look at ourselves through many others' eyes and get a "generalized view" of how others see us: the meaning that we have to these collective others. This ability to observe ourselves as a social status through the eyes of others can be more or less internalized in our mind as the "Me" that others see. Our social identity or self is a combination of both the inner "I" and the social "Me."

This social psychological insight has important implications for the process through which our identity remains stable or becomes trans-formed, which in turn has implications for the process of becoming deviant. Most of the time people behave in habitual or routine ways but, as Matsueda has said, when problems with others arise, we start to reflect on what went wrong. At such times: "The person takes the role of the other, views the problematic situation from the standpoint of significant others, and evaluates alternative lines of action from the perspective of others" (Matsueda, 2001: 234). When a satisfactory solution is reached, the person may change his or her behavior to reduce those problems and conflicts. In this sense, the person may be said to have exercised self-control, but in effect has been subject to social control. As a result, we can see that "the self arises through role-taking, the process of taking the role of the other, viewing one's self from the perspective of the other, and controlling one's behavior accordingly . . . Moreover, because role-taking involves considering lines of action from the stand-point of reference groups, it follows that behavior is controlled by social groups. Self-control is actually *social* control" (2001: 224).

Whether we decide to conform to the view others have of us, by adjusting our behavior to fit their expectations, or whether we resist, or ignore what we perceive, can be critical factors in the process of becom-ing deviant. Clearly, if we don't adjust, because we can't empathize, or because we are so blinded by our sense of injustice about our own situ-ation, or because of narcissistic tendencies that focus everything back on ourselves, then we risk drawing more negative heat about our behavior/ideas/appearance. As we have seen in the case of Robbie, for whatever reason, he was unable or unwilling to change. Instead, his anger brought more attempts at control, which brought more anger, and ultimately, even though he occupied a series of semi-normal roles, he was fragile, volatile, unstable, and explosive. For others, adjustment or defiance might be a more subtle process.

While altering our behavior in accordance with our sense of our social self, we are also changing who we are or at least who we are seen to be. We may genuinely want to become the person whom others see us as, or we may simply want to manipulate the way others see us by presenting our social selves as a package of how we want to be seen. We engage in a variety of symbolic communication that sociologist Erving Goffman (1959) variously called "impression management," "strategic interaction," and "role distancing," or similar social manipulation designed to convince others that what they see is "really" us. However, since we know that we are managing impressions, and we know, in the case of those experimenting with deviant behavior, that we have been engaging in banned behavior, this can give rise to problems of "secrecy," concealing the facts of deviant behavior, and "transparency," especially the fear that we may be seen for who we really are. This raises the question for us of who we really are: who is the real me?

> The problem of transparency . . . is that others may see through the subject's flimsy attempts to conceal the fact that s/he has misbehaved . . . The subject has to appear conventional . . . To do this, the subject has to be devious – s/he has to play at being ordinary. The irony is that, having exerted so much effort to appear ordinary, the subject performs a self-disservice by glimpsing the possibility that s/he is, after all, only playing at it. (Box, 1981: 211)

Such self-doubt prepares the way for the identity transformation that produces secondary deviance: that is, the identity transformation in which a person comes to believe that they are or have a deviant identity rather than a person who acts deviantly. Again, this is not a two-step process, but one that is progressive over time. If this process plays out, the deviant activity can come to overwhelm a person's life as they become engulfed by their deviant identity.

An important issue that is especially significant for the transformation from social deviance to deviant identity is the relative strength of our own individual sense of self, relative to our sense of the social selves that we internalize as a result of role-playing the generalized views held of us by others. Some people have a strong sense of who they are, regardless of others' views of them; others have a weak sense of who they are and are more vulnerable to the influence of others. In the case of those with visible forms of deviance, the effects of audience reaction on the person's sense of social self can be devastating. Consider the humiliating experience of some short people:

> It is not unusual for a person to stand on a bus or train rather than to sit next to a person of restricted growth. One member was humiliated by a woman refusing to use a toilet cubical she had vacated. This sort of thing tends to erode one's dignity. *If you don't have a strong character, it can be quite devastating.* I know people who will shut

themselves indoors for a week after a bad experience. (A. Brown, cited by Robinson and Henry, 1977: 48)

Bowlby's attachment theory suggested that parenting is a critical component in developing secure selves, resistant to the dominance of others' definitions of our selves. We saw how years of childhood abuse by parents, as in the case of Robbie, or by peers at school in the case of rampage school shooters, can have destructive outcomes. Obviously these are the exceptions, but they are extreme ends of a continuum. In between, there are numerous children who go through some, but not all, of these experiences to become potential deviant identities. Whether they become actual deviants, in the sense of secondary deviants locked into their deviant identity, depends on the combination of their biography and environment and on the social processes that intercede. For many, it could go either way. So how does one acquire or achieve a deviant social status?

Deviant social status and social stereotypes

A deviant status is one assigned to an actor by an audience on the basis of the meaning they hold of the ideas, behavior, or attributes held by the actor. Essentially, it is a judgment about the moral worth of a person based on the social meaning of certain characteristics. The judgment is expressed in a shorthand fashion by a category, label, or stereotype. Since it is assumed that ideas and behaviors are chosen, and an alternative non-deviant behavior could have been chosen instead, deviant statuses arrived at in this way are known as "achieved." In contrast, those deviant statuses relating to an actor's qualities or attributes that they are born with, such as race, gender, dis/ability, are known as "ascribed." In a sense they are both ascribed, since any differences first have to be perceived by an audience and given meaning in order to be later judged as significant. However, in the case of achieved deviance, the actor is seen as being partly, if not wholly, responsible for their behavior and the audience's use of labels, whereas in the case of ascribed status, this is not necessarily so. Where physical conditions are deemed negative attributes, those who possess them are stigmatized and become subject to social exclusion:

Many disabilities – blindness, deafness, mental retardation, paraplegia, and the like – were held to so thoroughly permeate all facets of sufferers' lives, that they constituted a decisive factor in virtually everything the individuals did and thus became their master status. In this way, people with disabilities were defined as different from (and less than) others. They were classified as abnormal and were subjected to various forms of treatment, discrimination, institutionalization, and exclusion. (Hanson, 2000)

A person may achieve or be ascribed to more than one deviant status, and these may be core or peripheral to their lives. A core or "master status" is one that takes precedence over all others that a person possesses, such that the person comes to represent the thing described. At the same time, all their other statuses are consumed by their master status. Consider the following account by a person describing her sense of self while being obese:

> I became very aware that I was unattractive when I was fat and it made me very, very miserable . . . It meant that when I was fat, wherever I went, I was not conscious of being a woman, nor of being a nothing, or of being something, or of being a friend, or of being a stranger. I was conscious of being a fatty and I felt ugly . . . Day and night for years it got me that bad. (Robinson and Henry, 1977: 49)

A peripheral or "auxiliary status," by contrast, is the expected behaviors, ideas, or attributes of someone possessing a master status. As might be expected, it is usual that the moral standing of both the master and auxiliary statuses are seen as inferior. Consider, for example, HIV/AIDS. Because of the fear of the disease, and because the disease has been associated with some deviant behaviors, those diagnosed with HIV/AIDS fear revealing their condition because the diagnosis may lead to these auxiliary negative statuses:

> [B]ecause HIV/AIDS is associated with marginalized behaviors and groups, all individuals with HIV/AIDS are assumed to be from marginalized groups and some may be stigmatized in a way that they were not before. For example, in some settings, men may fear revealing their HIV status because it will be assumed that they are homosexual. Similarly, women may fear revealing their serostatus because they may be labeled as "promiscuous" or sex workers and stigmatized as such. Second, HIV/AIDS exacerbates the stigmatization of individuals and groups who are already oppressed and marginalized, which increases their vulnerability to HIV/AIDS, and which in turn causes them to be further stigmatized and marginalized. (Parker and Aggelton, 2002: 4)

Although the sudden declaration that one has HIV/AIDS seems to instantly confer deviant and associated statuses, the assimilation of a deviant status does not generally happen instantly. To become a secondary deviant, the actor must accept the deviant label that the audience seeks to confer, and the audience needs to further respond to the person whose moral standing is in question. This is an iterative process. The audience's contribution to the development of a person's deviant status is to increase the formality, force, and frequency of its collective definition of the person as deviant. This can happen by primary, that is intimate, groups, such as family and friends, informally labeling a person as a particular type. Whether their definitions have a significant effect depends, as we've seen, on how sure a person is of their own identity. It also depends on the stage in life that these assertions of a person's identity occur. Up to ages 6 or 7, parents can be very influential; between 8 and 11, peers' views become predominant. Many parents report a transformation in their children by the time they enter middle school. By the time kids become teenagers, parents' views have been replaced by the school's views and peers' views, with the latter gaining in importance. The early teen is a conformist to the peer group and their worst nightmare is being seen as different, as we saw in the previous chapter. Difference subjects you to attention, gossip, and possible ridicule. According to the classical developmental psychologists' view, from ages 13 to 20 adolescents learn about their own self-identity, but also engage in minor delinquency. At this stage, adolescents have huge self-doubts, can be confused, and suffer feelings of anxiety and inferiority.

Clearly, participants in deviant activity do not necessarily see their behavior negatively, even if adults hold such a view. For example, a British study by the Social Issues Research Centre in 2004 found that "teenagers will present themselves in a certain way, through talking about drugs, supporting certain bands and adopting particular styles, to fit in with their group, or 'music tribe'" (SIRC, 2004: 3). The study identified ten current leading teenage music-based "tribes" in the UK – Academics/Geeks, Gangstas, Goths, Indies, Moshers, Scallies, Skaters, Sporties, Townies, and Trendies:

> Being part of a tribe allows us social inclusion and a means of identifying ourselves alongside those whom we look up to or aspire to emulate. It provides a social arena in which we can act out prescribed roles, adopting the appearance or style that serves as a representation of our allegiance. Modern tribes tend to select themselves by their cultural tastes and lifestyle choices. The mass media has given modern day communities a common context and language which can be used to determine today's teenagers' choice of tribe ... Within the teenage music tribes, there is a kind of alternative "career" structure in which social and personal identities are developed. At the "novice" stage in early teenhood, youngsters are looking for opportunities to blend in

with their friends or to stand out from other groups of teens in a "blended-in" kind of way. At around the ages of 14 or 15, issues such as personal appearance and dress style become more significant and it is at this stage that the desire to be associated with a particular genre of music is evident, in contrast to the mainstream pop that might have sufficed at an earlier age. This is when tribes start to form in earnest and it is when the peer group starts to be important in supporting young people, whose lives are often characterised by a mixture of confidence and excitement, coupled with distinct lack of self-belief. (2004: 5–6)

The British study found that boys were more likely, for example, to claim that they have taken drugs when they have not: "17 percent of 11–13 year-olds, 21 percent of 14–16 year-olds and 22 percent of over-16 year-olds think their friends pretend to have taken drugs when they haven't." Over half thought that young people over-claimed their drug use to "look cool" and "impress friends":

> The most self-aware and image-conscious group is that of the "Gang-stas," characterised by their love of hip hop stars like Eminem, sports brands and "bling." The Gangsta tribe is most likely to say that their taste in music influences their personal appearance, at 72 percent. They are also the most likely to "talk up" their drugs misuse, at 35 percent. This compared with an average of 23 percent within the 11–18 year-old age group, and 9 percent of Academics/Geeks and 19 percent of Scallies. (2004: 3)

In short, teenagers engaged in primary deviance represent a particular risk population for labeling and stereotyping by others, whether the labelers are their own peers, teachers, adults, or the school or juvenile justice system.

Stereotypes and categories

At the informal level, audiences already have a stock of socially constructed, stereotypical categories in which to place others. If no category is available, human ingenuity will exercise its creativity with flare. Stereotypes are categories that purport to capture the essence of a person according to key features that are drawn out as important. We all use stereotypes to negotiate our daily interaction, since to do otherwise would limit our ability to function: "Stereotypes are probabilistic beliefs we use to categorize people, objects, and events. We have to have stereotypes to deal with so much information in a world with which we are often uncertain and unfamiliar" (Yueh-Ting Lee, cited by Bower, 1996). We are taught to use stereotypes from childhood and we build up our stock of knowledge about the world through stereotypes about people. We learn much of that stereotypical imagery early, and often from peers rather than adults, although we also gain a significant portion from popular culture through the media. While evidence suggests that stereotypes have some core truths, when classifying problematic behaviors that are seen as threatening they tend to be exaggerations and contain distortion and misinformation. The informational content of the stereotypes is believed to be true by those using them, but is usually seen as a gross distortion of the truth by those being classified.

The audience works with these stereotypes, attempting to fit the suspected person into the deviant category. Anyone who engages in behavior prescribed by the category is liable for inclusion. However, who is chosen for stereotyping, particularly by more formal institutions and organizations, tends to reflect those in society with less power. Like the rule creation we examined in chapter 2, stereotyping is a social process reflecting the values and interests of those in positions of power:

> Whether or not the negative reactions have an impact (or become "sticky" to use a labeling term) is primarily determined by the relative power of the (potential) deviant(s) and the social audience. The relative power is determined by a number of factors such as the numbers in each group (deviant and reactors), the amount of wealth and income (property) of each group, the relative prestige of each group, the level of organization of each group (from individualized to subcultural to organized), and the relative quality of their discourse or claims (ability to persuade and manipulate symbols). These various sources of power interact in determining the ability of a given social group or audience to apply negative or positive labels to a type of behavior, condition, or particular group of (potential) deviants. Viewed in this light, deviant behavior is, in essence, a test of power relationships and serves as a potential threat to the power of the dominant group(s). (Heckert and Heckert, 2002: 468–9)

For example, in seeking to understand the process of stigmatization among HIV/AIDS sufferers, researchers have recognized that, rather than simply being a psychological process, stigmatization is a social and political process. Stigmatization and stereotyping are not just what some individuals do to others but are social processes, "linked to the actions and attitudes of families, communities, and societies" (Parker and Aggelton, 2002: 10). Indeed, stigmatization and discrimination are not isolated phenomena or the expression of individual attitudes, but are social processes used to create and maintain social control and to produce and reproduce social inequality. . . Stigma is something that is "produced" and used to help order society. For example, most societies achieve conformity by contrasting those who are "normal" with those who are "different" or "deviant." Cultures therefore produce "difference" in order to achieve social control . . . Similarly, concepts of symbolic violence and hegemony highlight the role of stigmatization in establishing social order and control, and identify stigmatization as part of the social struggle for power . . . Following from the notion that stigmatization is a process that involves identifying differences between groups of people, and using these differences to determine where groups fit into structures of power, is the idea that stigma and discrimination are used to produce and reproduce social inequality. Stigmatization, therefore, not only helps to create difference, but also plays a key role in transforming difference based on class, gender, race, ethnicity, or sexuality into social inequality. Stigmatization is also used by dominant groups to legitimize and perpetuate inequalities, and concepts of symbolic violence and hegemony can also help us understand how it is that those who are stigmatized and discriminated against so often accept, and even internalize, the stigma to which they are subjected. This is because the processes of symbolic violence and hegemony convince the dominated to accept existing hierarchies and allow social hierarchies to persist over generations, without generating conscious recognition from those who are dominated. In addition, these processes limit the ability of oppressed and stigmatized groups and individuals to resist the forces that discriminate against them. (Parker and Aggelton, 2002: 9–10)

Thus, once a person becomes subject to consideration for a deviant status, the audience, reflecting the political values of the wider social order, starts to reevaluate or retrospectively review and assess the past behavior of all those targeted for stigmatization in an attempt to determine whether or not it was an instance of the stereotypical character. Only those features of a person's past biography that are consistent with the public deviant status are noted. In like manner, the audience begins to anticipate behaviors, ignoring those that are not designated by the stereotype, and underscoring those that reaffirm it. At the same time the audience cuts off the actor from conventional behaviors and limits the types of activities that would confirm normality.

These processes occur once a person's ideas, behavior, or attributes are seen as sufficiently different and disturbing to warrant consideration of them as deserving of a deviant status. Some level of public knowledge of an actor's deviant activity is required for this to occur, since a deviant status is a socially constructed identity. However, there are clearly levels of public acknowledgment of potential deviant status that result in the deviant-making process discussed above.

At the most basic level is the process of self-labeling. This is "auto-suggestive," based largely on modeling one's behavior or whole personality on that of others. The way a person whose deviance is secret becomes subject to the deviant-making process is by them sharing in, and observing, publicly available stereotypes of deviants, and then by classifying themselves as such a person in conversations with themselves. Thus self-labeling requires:

> (1) knowledge of the social rules and their moral meanings, (2) self-acknowledgement that one has engaged in disapproved behavior, and/or (3) a sense of the low esteem in which such rule breakers are held. It assumes only that (1) the individual shares the dominant or popular definition of their behavior or condition, (2) that there are popular labels referring to such people, and (3) that the actor is generally motivated to conform to social norms . . . The rule violator may then proceed to label him/herself in ways consistent with public meanings. (Pfuhl and Henry, 1993: 170)

Acting as both labeler and labeled, the person may begin to restrict their own normal interaction to the company of those sharing the same attributes or behavior. Subsequent labeling by others may follow, but the major impetus for this labeling is the public existence of such a label. This begins by learning negative beliefs about certain kinds of deviance, and escalates through secrecy and concealment once official labeling kicks in. Interestingly, some adolescents may not want to conceal their deviance, as we've seen earlier, but instead seek to broadcast it. This is particularly true where the behavior in question has positive value among peers, even though, or even because, it has negative value among adults.

At a second level, public knowledge of the deviant activity may go beyond the group of fellow deviants to a nearby group who may begin an informal labeling process. These groups may include parents, peers, and teachers, who can begin an unofficial labeling process (Matsueda, 1992) and, because "the self is a reflection of appraisals made by significant others," such informal negative labeling "would influence future delinquency through the role-taking process" (Matsueda, 2001: 235). Role taking includes "learned definitions of delinquency, anticipated reactions to delinquency, and delinquent peers," which can move the role taker either in "a conventional direction (e.g. when taking the role of conventional groups) or a criminal direction (e.g., when taking the role of criminal groups)" (Heimer and Matsueda, 1994, cited by Matsueda, 2001: 235). Informal labeling starts earlier than formal and may continue in parallel with it.

Theory of office

Beyond this informal labeling, the deviancy-conferring process starts to become more institutionalized. Labeling of deviant behavior and stereotyping of persons as deviant can occur in secret or in public. Secret labeling occurs in any organized setting and has been described as "the theory of office." One example of this was discussed in chapter 1: when restaurant staff classified customers as normal ("tippers") or deviant ("stiffers"), and treated them accordingly, with self-fulfilling outcomes. Consider the revelations of these waitresses:

> The degree of personal satisfaction we get comes, in large part, from how we can "play" the customers, despite the restaurant rules . . . Lauren works the system of stereotypes to increase both her tips and the feeling of having done a good job. She looks at customers' physical appearance and partly at their dress in order to classify them. She feels if someone is dressed well and presents him or herself accordingly, then they'll have too much pride not to tip. "I also look at how receptive they are, their smile, their body language. Eye contact is important too . . . It shows that you're paying attention." . . . Jessica agreed that dress was important . . . the manner of dress showed whether a person cared enough about themselves to spend money. Speech distinguished those who had been educated from those who had not. She said ethnicity and social upbringing told her whether a person would know what a tip was . . . Tanya thinks that stereotyping and the resulting exclusion of those who are unable to speak and to represent themselves is necessary and justified: "I realize I am judging people but that is just so that I can find an effective way of dealing with them. After all, I wait on hundreds of people. You have to label them somehow or you'll go crazy." . . . Tanya goes out of her way to avoid those guests who appear to be overly curious and demanding and prefers men to women: "men are more easy-going because they are in the restaurant to enjoy themselves. Women are pickier because they are used to serving their husbands and expect the same from you as they expect from their family." (L. Miller, 1999: 48–9)

The theory of office refers to the way workers in institutions and organizations develop a rationale in order to fulfill their work task. Members of any organization dealing with the public and serving them as customers or clients are able to classify the behavior of those with whom they deal or serve. Most service workers have shared stereotypes of those that they serve, and these often involve both normal and deviant types. By classifying customers or clients, workers are able to bring order to an otherwise anonymous mass of the public. However, it is very rare that these organizationally developed stereotypes are shared with the people who are being labeled. People will be treated differently by such workers but will rarely know it because the workers keep up "a front." Erving Goffman's distinction between "front stage" and "back stage" is useful here, since the stereotyping by workers of their customers or clients goes on almost wholly in the "back stage."

Importantly, agencies whose institutional responsibility is to deal with populations of deviants, such as mental patients or delinquents, operate by classifying their clients into "normal" deviants and "deviant" deviants:

> the order created is not intended to enhance treatment or rehabilita-tion, but is designated to solve organizational problems, promote a smooth and efficient operation and protect the agency from criti-cism . . . The theory of office provides "recipes for action" that serve to routinize tasks. Included are typifications or standardized categories based on selected characteristics by which clients are classified . . . for routine handling and ease of processing. (Pfuhl and Henry, 1993: 132–3)

Knowing and implementing the routines includes classifying patients, clients, arrestees, etc., according to the shared meaning among the pro-fessionals or practitioners, a process that normalizes their behavior. Normal deviants are treated professionally, whereas deviant deviants are given special treatment. Workers in institutions charged with managing those who have been publicly designated as deviant apply their own informal and unofficial layering of deviant types in order to provide routine ways to handle this potentially more threatening group. In eth-nomethodologist David Sudnow's terms, these agency officials generate a range of "normal" to "deviant" deviants. At each stage of the public processing of persons suspected of deviance, we have this two-tier process of typing in operation: (i) labeling by agency workers, and (ii) labeling by the whole process. In effect, they have been classified as a deviant twice: by society, and by the agency workers in the bureaucracy.

A third level in the process of conferring deviant status occurs pub-licly through institutions and organizations specifically designated for that purpose; principally law enforcement agencies, the courts, and psy-chiatric screening boards. In the social construction of deviants, the courts process clients with the expressed purpose of deciding whether or not they have committed a certain-type of deviant activity and, further, whether a public, societal level of labeling is warranted. Ethnomethodologist Harold Garfinkel has described such public rituals, designed to significantly transform a person's identity into a lower moral status, as "status degradation ceremonies." During these processes, which typically take place in formal settings, such as a court, one's old identity is removed and a new one is conferred as the person undergoes a "status passage" or transition to their new identity. Indeed, the key issue is often not so much guilt or innocence but whether the person is the type of person capable of doing the behavior in question. The defense or advocate presents the person as favorable and normal, while the prosecution or accusers present the act as one typical of the kind committed by a certain type of deviant and presents a case that the person in question has just such a biography.

A fourth level of public labeling occurs with sentencing to confinement in a place such as a detention center, training school, special hospital, prison, etc., designed specifically for containing such persons. The most extreme versions of these are what Erving Goffman described as the "total institution." These are places requiring the complete subordination of the person, now labeled as deviant, segregating them physically and morally from non-deviants. In total institutions, all aspects of the client's former identity are removed, such as personal belongings and clothing, and they are issued with uniform clothing, and numbers rather than names. This results in a "mortification of the self" which creates a "spoiled identity." Here the agency workers' labeling and typing process is given legitimation because of the wider labeling process. As a result, the agency workers have little difficulty in revealing their labels and inflicting them upon those already publicly confirmed as deviants. The convergence of public and private deviant designations is the most powerful of audience statements about a person's moral identity.

In his classic research into the practices of in-patient psychiatric hospitals, entitled "Being Sane in Insane Places," psychologist D. L. Rosenhan sent eight people who had never had a diagnosis of mental disorder into twelve different mental hospitals on the east and west coasts of the United States. Their charge was to go to the mental hospital intake assessment area complaining of hearing voices. They were told to state that they were not currently hearing voices and, if asked by the intake psychiatrists to describe what the voices sounded like and what they said, they were to say they were muffled and unclear but sounded "empty," "hollow," and made a "thud," and the voices were of the same sex as the pseudo-patient. Other than this, all the information they gave to staff was the truth about who they were and what they did. Among these "pseudo-patients" were three psychologists, a psychiatrist, a student, a housewife, a painter, and a pediatrician, each with normal lives. Three were women and five were men. They were given pseudonyms, and those in mental health chose another occupation. If admitted to the hospital they were charged with observing and noting the way the staff treated the patients. Also, they were not to reveal their true purpose or the purpose of the research they were conducting, but were to act normally as sane individuals, to cease simulating any symptoms of abnormality, and to see how long and by what processes they were released. Only the hospital's chief administrator and chief psychologist knew what was occurring. If prescribed drug treatments, they were not to take the drugs.

To their surprise the pseudo-patients had no difficulty being admitted, with a typical diagnosis as being psychotic, possibly suffering from schizophrenia. Expecting to be released within a day or two when the hospital would find they were really sane, the pseudo-patients were shocked to find that they were committed from 7 to 52 days, with an average stay of 19 days! Moreover, once admitted they were treated like the other patients by the staff, which meant they were ignored as people since they were now classified as mentally ill. At first the pseudo-patients tried to conceal their note-taking for fear that it would reveal their true purpose, or at least cause questions to be asked. But they eventually realized that it didn't matter, since everything they did was seen as symptomatic of their newly designated status of "mental patient," "psychotic," or "schizophrenic." The staff reading of their behavior resulted in it being classified as symptomatic and translated into clinical jargon. The taking of notes, for example, was described in the clinical notes as "compulsive note taking." Patients who were lined up early waiting for their lunch or dinner were not seen as hungry, or anticipating the highlight of their otherwise boring and tedious day. One psychiatrist talking to a group of young residents "indicated that such behavior was characteristic of the oral-acquisitive nature of the syndrome. It seemed not to occur to him that there were very few things to anticipate in a psychiatric hospital besides eating" (Rosenhan, 1995: 292). Rosenhan says that, once given a psychiatric label, the qualities of the label served as a framework for interpreting the meaning of the person's behavior and their life events. Consider the case of one male pseudo-patient who had a close relationship with his mother, but was more remote from his father during early childhood – a pattern that reversed during adolescence when his father became a close friend and relations with his mother grew more distant; his relationship with his wife was close and warm, except for occasional angry arguments. His children were rarely spanked except when they were exceptionally naughty or defiant. In the psychopathological translation, the case notes on this "patient" stated:

This white 39-year-old male . . . manifests a long history of considerable ambivalence in close relationships, which began in early childhood. A warm relationship with his mother cools during adolescence. A distant relationship with his father is described as becoming very intense. Affective stability is absent. His attempts to control emotionality with his wife and children are punctuated by angry outbursts and, in the case of children, spankings. And while he says he has several good friends, one senses considerable ambivalence embedded in those relationships also. (1995: 291–2)

Rosenhan says that there was nothing ambivalent described in this pseudo-patient's relations with his wife, children, and friends, yet the facts of the case were unintentionally distorted so that they fit the contemporary theory of schizophrenic reaction. The ascribed meaning of his verbalized account as "ambivalence, affective instability" was determined by the diagnostic category of schozophrenia: "An entirely different meaning would have been ascribed if it were known that the man were normal" (1995: 292). The psychiatric staff retrospectively reinterpreted otherwise normal behaviors as indicative of the problem indicated by the label. Ironically, the other patients in the psych ward did detect that the pseudo-patients were sane, telling them: "You're not crazy. You're a journalist or a professor [referring to the continual note-taking]. You're checking up on the hospital!" (1995: 290)

One of the only means of psychological survival that persons can employ in such a total institutional setting is to distance themselves from fellow deviants through employing their own stereotyping of fellow designated deviants. The result is that it is possible for a person, subject to such a setting, to be labeled by: (i) fellow deviants in their struggle to survive; (ii) staff in their struggle to cope; (iii) the society in their attempt to contain and control; and (iv) their outside reference groups in an attempt to avoid contamination.

In summary, we have seen in this chapter how informal and formal processes of classification and deviancy designation shape and limit persons who behave deviantly, making them into people who are deviants. In the next chapter, we'll see how those designated as deviant respond to and cope with their deviant status.

6

Responding to deviant designations and coping with stigma

When I was a young girl in elementary school I was allowed to leave the room . . . five minutes early, go to the office and take five pills . . . I would then meet the rest of my class as they approached the lunch-room. To my peers I was lucky to be able to get out of class . . . To me, it was just something I had to do everyday before I ate anything. I had cystic fibrosis . . . The kids never knew, I never cared, and my disease went rather unnoticed . . . In response I was treated the same as everyone else.

In middle school my "difference" was given a name . . . it was obvious that adults had spread their "knowledge" about my condition and expressed to their children just how different I was from them. Admittedly, I was obviously different. I was far skinnier than any of the other girls. I coughed all year round . . . and I grew out of breath while running at PE or laughing too hard. My daily expedition to the office was now seen as strange rather than "neat." I was hospitalized several times during these years, which brought awareness to me, and my peers, about the seriousness of this "difference" between us . . . I began to feel different as a result, as the kids often looked at me as awkward or intimidating . . . Most still tried to be nice; some didn't, and wouldn't. I had friends, and continued to go to the "coolest" parties, but other than one best friend, no one attempted to come too close . . . During these years I realized, through the help of my peers, that I was different. I realized that not every child got up two hours before school to have therapy . . . and to do aerosol inhalers. I realized that not everyone took twenty pills a day and occasionally went to the hospital for weeks at a time. I realized that not everyone had another name like mine called something like cystic fibrosis.

I had been labeled as different, and had previously played into that role, believing I had no choice. But I no longer liked that role and felt a duty to step out of it . . . Once I made up my mind to change things, I began to look for ways to fit in. As I did this others followed my lead. I no longer felt so different, and as a result, others no longer saw me quite as different . . . The summer before my freshman year I decided that I wanted to be "cool." I wanted to be popular, pretty, and to have many, many friends. I knew that I would have to change people's perspective of me. I got in shape and tried out for the high school cheerleading squad with my friend from middle school. It was tough, especially for me, but we made it. I continued to cheer all four years, winning awards and even becoming captain. I went to most of the dances our school held, as I was also involved with all five sororities . . . I dated seriously, took trips with friends, and tried my hardest to be like everyone else, or better. I was still hospitalized numerous times and I continued to take pills every day, but my perception of myself threw a curve into everyone's perception of me.

I often got tired of the acting, even though I told myself it was positive thinking. Some people still looked at me strangely, asking . . . "Aren't you going to die before you turn eighteen? My mom told me you were." Most people though saw my desire to fit in and complied . . . I cheered. I partied. I dated, but I also took pills in secrecy, and coughed in the bathroom or behind muffled hands.

My label was wearing off. I was Staci and I did certain things because that's just who I was . . . For the most part I escaped their label, refused to accept their negative reactions, and went on to make a new person of myself . . . A few years after high school I underwent a lung transplant to "cure" my CF . . . Today I am "Staci, the girl with the transplant who is doing so well." It's two different lives, two different perspectives, and two different reactions from those who knew me before and those who know me now . . . I am still associated with that other (different) person I once was, but have succeeded in putting it in the past . . . Sometimes I miss that other person. I kind of see her as my little sister, someone to look out for and protect . . . Sometimes it's hard to be different, and difficult to escape the labels that are so quickly placed on you. Once seen as different it seems that you are always different – even if just a little bit . . . My condition was ascribed to me; my recovery was achieved by me. Unlike most deviants I was able to significantly succeed in rejecting my labeled identity given by the social reactions to my disease. Thanks to a positive attitude and a transplant "cure" I was able to change my deviant identity. (Wood, 1999: 137–41)

In this chapter we look at how those who are labeled "deviant" cope, react, or otherwise respond to being so labeled. In particular we look at the way people deal with the stigma associated with the negative label and with the stress accompanying the stigma. As Goffman (1963) noted, stigma designation constitutes a spoiled identity in the eyes of society, marking its bearer as less valuable, less complete, and less normal. A stigmatized person has been described as "a person whose social identity, or membership in some category, calls into question his or her full humanity – the person is devalued, spoiled, or flawed in the eyes of others" (Crocker, Major, and Steele, 1998: 504). As a result, stigma is the basis for experiencing shame, stress, and loss of self-esteem. A person's response to being publicly stereotyped with a negative deviant status can range from complete acceptance to complete rejection and all of the variations in between. In the example above, Staci went through a changing process over her life course, from her initial unwitting oblivion, to reluctant acceptance, and ultimate rejection as she successfully fought to establish herself as "the same" as anyone else, and in the process changed her peers' negative perception of her identity. Social psychologists who equate stigma with stress see the same coping mechanisms at play for both:

> One widely used coping inventory . . . identified 13 different ways people say they cope with events they appraise as stressful, including avoidance, denial, mental disengagement, behavioral disengagement, acceptance, positive reframing, venting negative emotions, seeking emotional support, seeking instrumental social support, religious coping, suppressing activities, active coping and planful coping. We assume that the responses of stigmatized persons to prejudice and discrimination are similar to the types of coping strategies people use in attempting to manage other types of stressful life events. (C. T. Miller and Major, 2000: 250)

Moreover, these researchers argue that the combination of effective coping strategies varies depending on the person, their goals, and their situation, including whether they have control over the source of the stigma creating their stress. People can strive harder to transcend the expectations associated with their stigma and become super-achievers, thereby individually solving their particular problem, as we can see in Staci's case. Alternatively, where they feel unable to change the way others perceive them, they may resort to coping emotionally with the consequences of others' reactions (2000: 250–1). As we saw in the previous chapter in the case of self-labeling, it is not even necessary to undergo the first stage of a stigmatization process, let alone every stage of public degradation, before a complete acceptance of the deviant identity occurs and before stigma coping strategies kick in. Conversely, a person might go through the whole private and public labeling and degradation process without capitulating to the label and its accompanying stigma:

> Rather than assuming that the experience of being stigmatized inevitably results in deep seated, negative and even pathological consequences for the personality of the stigmatized individual . . . people who are stigmatized experience a set of psychological predicaments, which they cope with using the same coping strategies as those used by the nonstigmatized people when they are confronted with psychological challenges such as threats to self-esteem . . . As a consequence there is considerable variation within stigmatized groups, just as there is within nonstigmatized groups . . . Current views . . . consider the processes of stigma to be highly situationally specific, dynamic, complex and nonpathological. (Dovidio, Major, and Crocker, 2000: 2)

For these reasons it is very difficult to empirically establish the contribution that audience labeling makes to the extent that the stigmatized accept a deviant status, as is testified by years of debate and conflicting evidence on this issue. Thus, in considering deviant outcomes, it is necessary to suspend judgment about what caused the level of acceptance of a label, and its associated stigma, and to look instead at the various responses actors have to being labeled.

Coping with deviant labels and stigma

In his classic study of stigma, Goffman (1963) made an important distinction between the "discreditable," whose deviance and/or stigmatized behavior or conditions are not publicly known, and the "discredited," where they are known or are unavoidable. The discreditable, also known as "secret deviants," would become discredited if their deviant identities were publicly known. If they are aware of their potential deviant designation, the discreditable can become very concerned with information management or passing among "normals" or "straights" so that their deviant behavior maintains its secrecy. In public, the discreditable attempt to pass as normal by avoiding symbols that give away their condition. They are engaged in cueing misinformation, adopting public lifestyles that mislead, or that lead one to construe an alternative impression. Clearly, devices and techniques of information management can be used by the discreditable, irrespective of whether they want to change their own identity or whether they want to continue the deviant behavior, appearance, or condition.

In the case of the discredited, the concern is very much with managing the effects of having a spoiled identity and attempting to minimize the stigma effects until such a time that the behavior or attributes have been transformed. The aim is to maintain a positive self-image. This has been described as a process of "normalization" or "deviance disavowal," in which the stigmatized acknowledge their devalued status but try to present a positive image of themselves. This may be achieved through de-stigmatization, in which the old stigmatized self is replaced by a new normal identity. It can be achieved by deliberate efforts to fit in, by super-moral action, voluntary work, or altruism. The person is, in effect, building up new moral credit. A positive self-image may also be achieved by transcendence, in which they achieve extraordinary success in a particular field of human endeavor. At the same time, deviant behavior in the person's life is increasingly replaced by new non-deviant behavior that gives rise to a new master status that drowns out the original stigmatized one. Here the person attempts to minimize the old deviant identity by pointing out that they are changing, that they have many more dimensions to their life than indicated by their past deviance, and that everyone has potentially stigmatizing problems.

Importantly, some deviants can, through their life course, move from discreditable through discredited, and finally emerge as recovered, as we saw in Staci Wood's example above. She began as a non-stigmatized, unaware deviant, whose behavior was not seen as significantly different; she became evidently different, saw herself as different, and was discredited as a result. But she rejected that negative label and its accompanying stigma by investing heavily in acting as and being normal. Importantly, this "deviance disavowal" involved a combination of both real accomplishment in normal valued activities and some concealment of symptoms of her stigmatized status. Ultimately she not only changed her socially stigmatized status, but also removed the physical cause of her stigma through surgery. She left most of her stigmatized identity in the past, though retains an appreciation for its significant meaning. Importantly, then, recovering discredited deviants still need to act as discreditable deviants in order to optimize the transformation of their stigmatized identity.

Discreditable deviance and the management of secrecy and stress

Controlling the information that reveals one's potentially stigmatized status is a major challenge for the discreditable deviant: "to display or not to display, to tell or not to tell, to let on or not to let on, to lie or not to lie; and in each case to whom, how, when and where" (Goffman, 1963: 42). One of the principal techniques is information diversion or deflection. This is an attempt by the deviant actor to deflect attention from revealing the act or condition in question on to some other issue to put it in a broader context, which dilutes its intensity, or to substitute a less stigmatized attribute for the more stigmatized one. In each case the objective is to change the meaning constructed of the situation. For example, some of the voluntary childless have been found to substitute the inability to have children for their decision not to have them, since the latter is more manageable: "The less stigmatized status of involuntary childless is presented to deflect the criticism that the voluntary childless status elicits and to end the conversation" (Park, 2006: 310). The displacement of one form of stigma by a lesser one is called "covering" (Goffman, 1963: 102–4).

The actor can also accomplish information management by putting on a performance to "pass" as a member of the accepted group. Faking or exaggerating one's positive values to the group questioning the behavior is one way of accomplishing information diversion through performance. High school males who fear that they are not going to fit into the dominant jock subculture may fake becoming more masculine than they are, or want to be, adding to the inflated image of the dominant group. As a result of such definitions of acceptability or unacceptability, and because of the fear of violent behavior for failing to conform, some boys in schools hide who they are:

> The boy who is good at sport, who is competent in the "right" kinds of work, and who can demonstrate his power over girls/women and other boys/men is the one who is likely to achieve recognition from his peers . . . However, these "achievements" do not come easily for most boys . . . The desire for manly successes, and consequent social respect, is also complemented by a fear of being one of the subordinated boys/men who provide a means by which other boys can assert their manliness . . . It is the possibility of attracting such attention that works to keep boys "in line" and to produce a silence among boys about issues of gender and violence. In order to not to attract such attention, boys have to distance themselves from any actions that may bring their masculine status into question. This often means that many idealized "manly" values are over-emphasized by those boys who have the potential or desire to achieve hegemonic masculine status and those who wish to avoid being the recipient of violence. Weaknesses have to be covered over, alignments with girls and subordinated boys need to be kept at a minimum and a commitment to hegemonic attributes

needs to be demonstrated at available opportunities. Fear therefore plays a major role in maintaining the gender order from inside challenges. This fear helps to perpetuate the normalization of violence as a masculine attribute. (Mills, 2001: 48–9)

Concealing one's self-identity in these ways, or being able to "pass" as a normal person by concealing one's stigmatized behavior or appearance can create its own problems. These problems include the actor's own belief that they are "a fraud," the inability to genuinely and openly connect to others in intimate ways, and the constant tension that the act of concealment produces. Indeed, "concealing a stigma leads to an inner turmoil that is remarkable for its intensity and its capacity for absorbing an individual's mental life" (Smart and Wegner, 2000: 221). Those who conceal their gay status from the straight world have demonstrated this in their expressions of relief in "coming out." Olympic diver Greg Louganis, who was both gay and tested HIV positive, expressed this concern. Prompted by a diving accident in the Seoul Olympics in which he hit his head on a board, Louganis was horrified at what his secret condition might do to others who were ignorant of it: "As he bled into the water and as doctors came to his aid, Louganis was overwhelmed with terror – not so much by his being hurt or by possibly losing his position in the competition, but instead by the fact that he was perhaps jeopardizing the lives of everyone who was coming in contact with his blood" (Smart and Wegner, 2000: 221). He later explained:

> I also want to set the record straight about who I am, because my secrets have become overwhelming. I want to start living my life the way normal people do, without having to watch every word, without having to remember what I've shared with whom. I want never again to feel compelled to hide out in my house in the California Hills, avoiding situations in which I have to edit what I say and lie about my life. (Louganis, 1995: xiii; cited by Smart and Wegner, 2000: 221)

Evidence suggests that, "as stigmatized people try to maintain secrecy about their stigmas, they become obsessively preoccupied with thoughts of their stigmas" (2000: 221–2). Part of their challenge and struggle is to deal with their suppressed negative feelings while being so preoccupied with the very issue making them who they are, creating them, which can create a "private hell," as has been demonstrated in studies of women with eating disorders who attempt to conceal their anorexia or bulimia (2000: 229–33). Similarly, studies of people with HIV-AIDS who try to conceal this information have shown the extent of emotional strain that is suffered: "As one man said 'I want to tell. I'm not used to hiding everything from everybody . . . I'm basically an honest person and I don't like to lie.' . . . A 33 year-old salesperson . . . said; 'I was at my desk and three secretaries telling AIDS jokes were standing right behind me. It cut and it hurt. I grit my teeth and said nothing'" (Weitz, 1993: 232).

These inner struggles clearly affect interaction with non-stigmatized others as they present further challenges that also need to be managed: "Conditions of ordinary social interaction that 'normals' take for granted often must be given considerable attention by those seeking to conceal their stigmatized conditions or behaviors" (Pfuhl and Henry, 1993: 195). For example, genital herpes sufferers have reported that normal interaction produces several situations, particularly dating situations, which trigger the topic and result in their investment of energy to conceal the problem: "It was a conscious effort to be the same old Thomas and to act the same way. And so I felt like I was just harboring a secret that no one was gonna get out of me" (Lee and Craft, 2006: 296). Another herpes sufferer said that she gets propositioned to dance at weddings: "I think about it then. I think like: If you only knew you wouldn't be asking me to dance" (2006: 296). Indeed, "Having a concealable stigma may affect the types of social relationships in which stigmatized people choose to become involved; for example they may opt for shallow relationships in which hiding is relatively easy . . . while people with concealable stigmas may appear at ease in an interaction, they experience deep cognitive activation of their stigmas" (Smart and Wegner, 2000: 235–6). Genital herpes sufferers report: "I go out of my way to avoid . . . dating-type situations." However, "through concealing the disease and withdrawing from relationships, the person with genital herpes protects himself or herself from losing affiliation with others" (Lee and Craft, 2006: 297). Thus, by curtailing some interactional situations, the secret deviant can maintain others, depending upon the nature of their stigmatizing condition.

Another way in which this is managed is to divide oneself into two people by leading a double life; one "in which severe restrictions are placed on one's choice of associates and friends . . . to resolve the tensions and anxieties that accompany unrestricted intermingling" (Pfuhl and Henry, 1993: 194). Research suggests three ways that the inner tension can be managed or forgotten for those with concealable stigmas: (1) automatic conscious mental control from practice; (2) situation management through avoiding situations that force faking and aligning instead with those who share the stigmatizing condition; and (3) redefining the stigma as not part of themselves, part of their former but not current selves (Smart and Wegner, 2000: 238–9).

Rose Weitz (1993: 232) showed that successful management also requires learning to anticipate how others may react and "learning when to tell." Indeed, the issue of when to tell or reveal the secret has been a constant theme for the discreditable deviant. Cystic fibrosis sufferer Staci describes how initially she was engaged in "selective concealment," deciding who was "worthy" to tell: "I knew, especially while younger, that some kids would make fun, while others would accept me as one of them. It was often hard to decipher between the two" (Wood, 1999: 141). She also found it helpful to use "therapeutic disclosure," whereby she would talk to doctors, relatives, and friends, "allowing me the freedom to be myself, cough hard, or perhaps grow out of breath" (1999: 141). All of this may also require the assistance of knowing others, such as doctors, family members, and trusted friends, in a conspiracy of silence: "In such cases people tacitly agree to preserve the fiction that there is nothing different or unusual about the deviant or his or her actions" (Pfuhl and Henry, 1993: 196). For example, in the case of people with HIV-AIDS, doctors could achieve this concealment on behalf of their patients by manipulating the diagnosis (Weitz, 1993: 230). Cystic fibrosis sufferer Staci employed "preventative disclosure" to "warn teachers, very close friends, PE coaches and neighbors of my illness in case I needed to leave class to get water, wanted to have friends spend the night or if I had to unexpectedly go to the hospital" (Wood, 1999: 141). This would enable her friends to cover for her in advance, so that others would remain unaware.

Although "counterfeit secrecy" can reinforce the idea of one's unacceptability, promote self-alienation, and "serve as the basis for erecting barriers between self and others from whom one might conceivably obtain emotional support" (Pfuhl and Henry, 1993: 197), others have found that revealing the secret can have several positive outcomes. In their study of genital herpes sufferers, Lee and Craft found that there were several reasons why the discreditable allowed themselves to become discredited. They say that genital herpes respondents "tell because: (1) others are predisposed to accept them, (2) telling is demanded by the relationship's character; (3) the secret is getting in the way of a valued relationship." They say: "our findings move us beyond our expectation, demonstrating that threats of losing relationships because of secrecy and withdrawal may also prompt revelations to save relationships" (Lee and Craft, 2006: 298). Importantly, these researchers found that there is also a self-identity component, such that "respondents reveal a desire to tell others so that having genital herpes does not change who they are; their previous selves are not lost to the disease when they find people who accept them," and this "fulfills their need for self-verification" (2006: 298). They conclude:

Effective stigma management is a social process. Those coping better with genital herpes are the ones who can tell others about suffering disapproval. Finding support within existing social networks, or creating support in new networks, seems key to overcoming adverse effects of stigmatization. Persons without opportunities for acceptance risk damaging personal consequences or dramatically changed social lives. (2006: 302)

Discredited deviance and the management of self, situations, and others

As stated at the outset of this chapter, there are several responses to the force of negative labeling resulting from stereotypes. In the case of visible stigmas, some of the same coping mechanisms of avoidance that are used by the discreditable may come into play. As we saw in Staci's opening example, in an effort to preserve their own self-identity those engaging in deviant behavior, or displaying deviant attributes, may not readily acquiesce to the view that one aspect of their life determines their whole social and moral identity, especially if that identity is judged negatively to be inferior. Many designated deviants do not even entertain that their activity is deviant, in spite of others' statements to the contrary. Those who avoid the labeling process may do so by not accepting the possibility that what they do or how they appear is wrong or morally reprehensible. In its purest form, such avoidance does not address negative evaluations; it simply ignores them. In other forms, actors acknowledge the existence of negative stereotypical labels but engage in a variety of dramaturgical skills and techniques in which they endeavor to renegotiate, excuse, and otherwise recast the meaning of their behavior to create a new moral identity.

One strategy to compensate for these problems is for the stigmatized to excel in areas in which the stigma would suggest their performance or ability would be limited. This may involve the exertion of extraordinary effort, refined skills, and developed assertiveness. The objective here is to show that the discredited person is "not like other people in the stigmatized group" (C. T. Miller and Major, 2000: 254). Another strategy is to challenge the audience's view that the discredited person's status or condition limits their range of possible behaviors. Staci employed just such a "normalization" technique: "I strived to be the best at everything I did, especially athletic activities. I relied on exercise to normalize myself with others of my age. I water-skied, swam and cheered, all to my fullest capabilities. I thought that these activities would blend me in with everyone else. I was correct in that assumption" (Wood, 1999: 142).

Another strategy is to remove the cause of the stigma, which Staci eventually did by having lung transplant surgery; as those who are overweight do by losing weight, even to the extent of having Bariatric surgery; and as others do through various kinds of therapy for mental disorder or substance abuse (C. T. Miller and Major, 2000: 252–3).

However, because the discredited person is not able to conceal their stigma, instead of striving to transform others' views of it, some try to appeal to the audience for special accommodation. For example, deviant actors whose behavior is in question may try to draw on their bank of moral credit, asking the immediate audience to consider overlooking their questionable behavior, in the light of their past behavior. However, this accommodation could also be lost if the deviance from group norms persists over time. This is similar to the "metaphor of the ledger," and can be used as an apologia and as part of an appeal to be given another chance, with the implication that the behavior will not happen again. For example, in his observations on the pressure from fellow students to go out drinking, Vincent came under moral pressure to conform to the normative behavior of the group, albeit the deviant one from society's point of view – that of student binge drinking or "partying":

> When I shook off the efforts of my friends to get out (and party) they said, "Some friend you are," and that I was weak and then they waited to see if I would fold. But I never experienced any long-lasting stigma when I stayed at home and my friends went out. I would see their disapproval and did not like it but I was able to dish it out. I noticed that staying in on Friday night and "catching shit" was quickly forgotten on Saturday night when I went out and drank beers with my friends. However, I was made to feel badly for what I had "missed" the night before. It became evident to me that it was only when one does not go out drinking several times in a row that a person will receive the label "pussy." Once one has been out of the group for a while it is not easy to get back in. (Vincent, 1999: 97)

One of the classic accommodation coping techniques is the excuse. Excuses, as we saw in the previous chapter, are statements in which the actor accepts that the activity is wrong but denies full responsibility for it. Excuses are attempts to repair the broken social relations resulting from the deviant activity or appearance. Excuses include denying responsibility, either by claiming that there are larger forces with which a person has to contend, or by claiming that they were not themselves at the time. A variety of different forms of excuses are available and may be accepted or "honored" by the audience. For example, Vincent found that his alcohol buddies accepted certain excuses for not partying as more legitimate than other excuses:

> There are certain legitimate excuses, even among friends. These are accepted as good reasons for not going out and can be used to relieve the pressure to participate in drinking. One of these is having a girl-friend. Chris felt the pressure placed on him to go out with the guys is much less effective because he has a girlfriend . . . He says it is easier to swallow the pressure from guys because they are much quicker to "forgive him" for going out with his girlfriend . . . Chris says he feels more likely to give in to pressure when he is just sitting around doing nothing than when he has to do something particular, like study for a test. (1999: 99)

Instead of excusing or apologizing for their deviant behavior and seeking the indulgence of the audience, some discredited deviants seek to solve their own emotional problems from the stigma by minimizing its effect. Ironically, one way of doing this is to compare themselves with similar others in worse situations than themselves in a downward comparison. This is a form of "scapegoating," which can itself stigmatize others. In its most pernicious form it has been defined as a

> discrediting routine by which people move blame and responsibility away from themselves and towards a target person or group. It is also a practice by which angry feelings and feelings of hostility may be projected, via inappropriate accusation, towards others. The target feels wrongly persecuted and receives misplaced vilification, blame and criticism; he is likely to suffer rejection from those who the perpetrator seeks to influence. (The Scapegoat Society, 2003)

Scapegoating produces an upward elevation of the deviant's own moral standing as relatively better-off. In contrast, a person with a deviant stigma may compare themselves with advantaged similar others, which provides hope that their own situation may improve in the future (C. T. Miller and Major, 2000: 258).

An alternative response to deviant designation, and its accompanying stigmatization, is acceptance and self-denial. Some of those who engage in deviant behavior, and are subject to the labeling process, accept the audience's definition but do not feel they are able to do anything about their behavior or their situation. They feel isolated and alone and respond to their deviant identity by becoming depressed, losing any sense of self-worth, and by "dropping out." People responding in this way feel considerable guilt at their own bedevilment and, even though they may engage in minimal attempts to conceal their deviant identity through secrecy and information control, they are unable to escape this obsession with their own transparency as a deviant. In such a situation, all the responses of others are scrutinized for any meaning indicating rejection. Even the normal responses of others are inverted and transformed into a reflection of the actor's own negative self-image. What others would take as part of the backcloth of social life is significant to the self-denying deviant because it is pregnant with the very problem the person experiences, as illustrated by the following comment by an involuntary childless sufferer: "You feel the world is full of other people's children. Wherever you go it's people with prams [strollers] . . . However good your friends are that have got children, there's just some things that obviously they'll really never understand. However much they try to understand you can't help but feel . . . resentment toward them. You try not to" (Robinson and Henry, 1977: 55).

As with the discreditable, the discredited may seek avoidance of the very situations and interactions that produce problems related to their stigma. Beyond avoidance and requests for accommodation, an alternative response to deviant designation is to reject the label and engage in individualized counter political action. Thus, rather than deny responsibility, those who see others reacting negatively to their behavior or condition may assertively reject the label and act to change it: "Discredited and discreditable, alike, may redefine their stigma as a positive attribute, resulting in pride rather than shame. In this case there is no longer a need to conceal their stigma; rather it is often flaunted" (Heitzig, 1996: 350). For example, some voluntary childless challenge the value of parenthood and claim that alternatives have greater value. They do so by challenging the taken-for-granted assumption that having kids is valuable, and argue that child rearing through other means, such as teaching, social work, foster care, or adoption, provides a great contribution to society since it is not adding to the overpopulation problem. In these situations the voluntary childless challenge parents to justify their choice to have children or assert the social value of childlessness by providing "evidence of social nurturance, workplace productivity, public resource support, or environmental responsibility" (Park, 2006: 313). In the process, they simultaneously diminish the stigma attached to their status.

Clearly what is resisted individually can also be resisted collectively through banding together with fellow deviants, in what Edward Sagarin (1969) described as "Odd Man In." I will discuss this in more detail in the next chapter. Before doing so, it is important to qualify this discussion about the effects of stigma and people's response to it.

Positive deviance

As I've made clear, much of the sociological literature on deviant designations makes the assumption that the experience of being labeled is negative. Those negatively labeled are seen as responding to, and coping with, the stigma or "spoiled identity" that negative labeling confers. However, while this is a significant part of the deviance process, it does not capture the whole story. In the special case of "positive deviance," coping with stigma is not an issue.

As stated previously, positive deviance is deviance that departs from social norms in positive ways: positive deviance signifies "positively sanctioned overconformity" (A. Heckert and Heckert, 2004: 209; 2002). The concept has been used in many contexts, such as to explain why some people within the same negative health environments, such as poverty, survive in good health and succeed, whereas most others are negatively afflicted. Positive deviance has also been used in the context of business and organizational studies, to explain how, in contrast to negative organizational deviance such as theft, sabotage, or incivility, there are intentional acts of extreme excellence when members deviate from organizational norms through honorable behaviors that would be positively evaluated by those defining the norms of the organization and that can, and often do, produce a major benefit to the individuals and organizations involved (Spreitzer and Sonenshein, 2004). The interesting question from the perspective of social deviance arises when the collectivity's norms, values, and existence are incongruent with those of the rest of society, yet they are admired in the deviant subgroup, conforming to its norms, and sometimes are also admired by members of the wider society (e.g. Robin-Hood-type villains or Bonnie-and-Clyde-type bank robbers). Indeed, in the case of deviant organizations, in spite of the negative view held by social controllers in the wider society, exceptional deviance within deviant groups is celebrated as "positive deviance" by those labeled deviant, not least because it is deviant *from* those norms of the wider society. In cases such as rebellion or protest groups: "deviance admiration designates positively reacted to underconformity (or nonconformity)" (A. Heckert and Heckert, 2004: 209; D. Heckert, 1998). Indeed,

> Social categorization of people into outgroups (different from the self) and in groups (including the self) stimulates a motivation to perceive or achieve a sense of positive group distinctiveness . . . this motivation can initiate a search for dimensions on which the ingroup is favored over the outgroup (and to placing greater emphasis on these dimensions), and it can also motivate active discrimination against outgroups

(which reflects positively on collective as well as personal self-esteem). (Dovidio, Major, and Crocker, 2000: 8)

However, as mentioned throughout, contexts have to be considered, since audiences can react to the same behavior or conditions in different ways. Positive deviants, as demonstrated by geeks, or gifted and over-achieving students, are "rate busters to their peers at the same time they are positive deviants to their teachers. Elite tattoo collectors are simul-taneously positive deviants to their subculture and negative deviants to the dominant society" (A. Heckert and Heckert, 2004: 213). So one strategy for dealing with stereotypical labeling is acceptance and embrace-ment of the stigmatized label, leading to a positive rather than negative self-esteem. Indeed, it is not uncommon for the labeled to interpret their labels as a reward for their efforts, rather in the manner that a college student receives a degree or a Hollywood actor receives an Oscar. It is said that such deviant actors are engulfed by the role, but this denies that they actually attempt to achieve it. What is certain is that some of those designated "deviant" strive to extend and expand their deviant status, developing a commitment to other deviant activity that would further enhance it and accept the inevitability of their deviant career. Instead of forming groups to share the problems associated with con-fronting a hostile audience, these actors form groups to practice the activity and engage in further attempts to conceal it, resulting in "devi-ancy amplification"; it is almost as if the social reaction to their behavior encourages further development of it and affirms their desired deviant identity. Consider the case of anorexics who desire the qualities of super-thinness:

> These girls don't see anything wrong with their behavior ... They don't feel they have a problem ... They have this elation which I have compared to being high on cannabis. Quite a lot of them have "smoked" and they say that when they are very, very thin, they have the same feeling as they have when they've been smoking. . . . They enjoy being thin; in fact nothing makes them happier. One of them said she loved nothing better than seeing her bones sticking out of her flesh. . . . While they are starving, they are in perfect control over their whole being. It's not just controlling their weight; it's controlling their lives and everything about them. So they are very happy. (Robinson and Henry, 1977: 47–8)

It is important to recognize, then, that deviants can gain positive value from their peers, and rather than merely "cope with" their deviant des-ignations, they can bask in the glory of their achieved deviant status, while others valued positively by society can suffer at the hands of their peers, as we saw in extreme in the case of the stigma attached to high school students who were made to feel worthless by the dominant high school subculture.

Finally, a related consideration is the variability of others' reactions to stigma. While there is a collective negative reaction to persons so designated, this is not the sum total of others' reactions. Indeed, some persons provide support, others might be intrigued, and yet others think the behavior or condition shows a positive, if socially misunderstood, strength. In order to determine others' likely reactions, some discreditable deviants, for example, explore the possible responses of others to their condition. Consider the account of a cancer patient:

> The whole question of the stigma around cancer – you had to break it down. There is a certain leper image to it born from the patient's point of view and the public . . . To be told that one, or a member of one's family, has cancer, conjures up the most dreadful fear, shock and worry. People drop their voices and whisper because associated with the word "cancer" is pain and death, something not to be spoken about. . . . [To avoid the stigma effects] I tried it out on people. I tried it out on the deliveryman, on the garage where I took my car to be repaired. When I told them . . . you could see this sort of expression on their face not knowing what to do or say. I felt sorry for them actually. (1977: 48, 53)

As with the meaning of labeling, so with the meaning of stigma, it can be highly dependent on situation and context (Dovidio, Major, and Crocker, 2000: 2–3).

In this chapter we have seen both the variety of ways in which people are designated with a deviant identity, and how they cope with the stigma attached to such deviant designation. In the next chapter we will see how people so designated join together with others for both mutual support and collective resistance.

7

Becoming normal: the politics of stigma

In the previous chapter we examined the many ways that individuals cope with the tension and anxiety stemming from their negative experience of being labeled as something less than normal, or with the knowledge that, if their behavior or condition were revealed, negative experiences would follow. We have seen that some of those designated as deviant cope through a variety of techniques designed to manage information and impressions of themselves. Through these processes they are able to achieve a significant, and often dramatic, recasting of the meaning that others hold regarding them. However, for others, individual coping responses may be inadequate, too daunting, or in some cases, too accommodating of the society, or the subgroups of society, that create the stigmatizing categories in the first place. Thus rather than struggle to "fit in," some of those labeled as social deviants join with their fellow discredited peers, either informally or in a variety of self-help, mutual aid, or advocacy groups. These groups of fellow deviants provide a shared sense of relief, a redefinition of the problem, and a series of activities designed to transform their situation through political and activist campaigns. Such resistance to being stigmatized as deviant can involve engagement in public stigma contests, conflict games, and counter protests. Those joining or founding these organizations of fellow deviants do so for a variety of reasons, and the organizations themselves have a variety of objectives. Some are dedicated only to providing collective support for their members; others believe they are entitled to challenge that which is taken to be normal and to engage in the political struggle over what counts as deviance, and what should be done about it. These are deviants who engage in politically organized activity to publicly change the views of the rest of society so that those who are influential at defining behavior will come to accept what they do. In this chapter, then, we will briefly explore the politics of *redefining* deviance from the perspective of the stigmatized. We will look at the ways in which groups of people sharing similar problems support members, and at the ways they challenge society and public policy.

Mutual aid for moral problems

We saw earlier that deviants may join together with others in groups, gangs, or other organizations to further their own deviant activities: "Typically their members, who are recruited from individuals rejected by society, are rarely concerned with the problematic nature of their stigmatized status but with developing, reaffirming and enlivening their deviant practices" (Pfuhl and Henry, 1993: 210). In such groups deviants can conceal their activities from public scrutiny, protect their members from discovery, share knowledge and skills, earn prestige and honor, and operate without confronting censure or sanction. As we saw in the previous chapter, the more deviant they are in their groups, the more likely they are to be celebrated for their "positive" deviance, at least from the perspective of the group (although this depends upon the nature of their deviance, since some will be deviant both to the society and to the deviant group, and be excluded and sanctioned by both). In such a context, deviants have little need to manage images or to "pass" in the wider society, although, ironically, they may have to exaggerate their own "badness" in order to stay strong in the group; fundamentally, such groups do not care what society thinks about what they do.

In this chapter we are more concerned with groups and organizations formed by deviants to support fellow deviants who are explicitly concerned with what society thinks about them and about their problems. They are concerned because they want to provide support to fellow problem sufferers by providing coping skills and expert knowledge, and/or they are concerned to change the views society holds of them and people like them. In joining such groups, those subject to stigma seek: "either (1) to conform to the norms of society, or (2) to change those norms to include the acceptance of his [or her] own behavior. In the first instance the person renounces deviant behavior, in the second he [or she] changes ... the rule making order" (Sagarin, 1969: 21). These groups are variously described as self-help or mutual aid groups and are of two types. "Inner focused groups" are oriented to service provision for their members, whereas "outer focused groups" are oriented to changing the public definition of their members' behavior or condition from "deviant" to "different," through public campaigns. While these are extremes, most self-help or mutual aid groups combine both inner and outer focused activities albeit with an emphasis towards one end or other of the continuum. For example, even the organization dedicated to reforming marijuana laws, NORML (The National Organization for the Reform of Marijuana Laws), provides members with helpful services, including legal support.

The second half of the twentieth century saw a phenomenal growth in self-help and mutual aid groups for people with a whole variety of modern problems, and particularly problems in which stigma attached to the behavior or condition. There were groups for people with alcoholism, drug abuse, mental disorder, obesity, anorexia, bulimia, childlessness, homosexuality, sexually transmitted disease, cancer, disabilities, and many, many more:

> The movement includes Parents Anonymous, Emphysema Anonymous, Overeaters Anonymous, Debtors Anonymous, Pill Addicts Anonymous, California Smokers Anonymous, Gamblers Anonymous, Depressives Anonymous, Prison Families Anonymous, Impotence Anonymous, Cocaine Anonymous, WWL2M (Women Who Love Too Much) and thousands of others . . . The groups, which exist for almost any problem, usually subsist on a shoestring, with nominal contributions from members, and range from those involving relatively few people – such as NO SAD, a . . . group for those with Seasonal Affective Disorders, or POND, for Parents of Near Drowners – to those with a broader reach, like Mended Hearts, for people who have had heart surgery, or Children of Aging Parents. . . . The groups are armed with talk-show relevancy and increasingly creative acronyms. There is JACS, for Jewish Alcoholics, Chemically Dependent Persons and Significant Others, and Female, for Formerly Employed Mothers at Loose Ends . . . Share, for Self-Help Action and Rap Experience. And their adherents see them as a grass-roots citizens' initiative. (Brown, 1988)

In 1976 Katz estimated there were some 500,000 different groups in the United States embracing several million members (Katz and Bender, 1976; Katz, 1981: 129); by 1988 "In North America, membership in self-help organizations has risen to an estimated 12 million to 15 million people" (Brown, 1988). Before the Internet became widely available, newspapers regularly contained lists of locally based groups that offered support for problem sufferers, holding regular meetings and developing member-relevant projects and activities; since the Internet and widespread web access, the ability to connect and communicate with self-help groups has been vastly improved, and numerous self-help clearing houses exist, through which people can find self-help groups for their problem or issue in their area. For example the American Self-help Clearinghouse is a "keyword-searchable database of over 1,100 national, international, model and online self-help support groups for addictions, bereavement, health, mental health, disabilities, abuse, parenting, caregiver concerns and other stressful life situations. It also lists local self-help clearing-houses worldwide, research studies, information on starting face-to-face and online groups, and a registry for persons interested in starting national or international self-help groups" (NJ and American Self-Help Clearinghouse, 2006). Indeed, the National Self-Help Clearinghouse, which was founded in 1976 by the late Frank Riessman who developed the "helper therapy principle" (the idea that those who give help to others benefit most from the relationship) (Riessman 1965), illustrates that even a clearinghouse provides services "to facilitate access to self-help groups and increase the awareness of the importance of mutual support." The Clearinghouse lists its goals as follows:

> Assists human service agencies to integrate self-help principles and practices into their service delivery. Conducts training activities for self-help group leaders and for professional facilitators of support groups. Provides consultation to public agencies to promote their capabilities to encourage and sustain mutual support groups. Carries out research activities, including research about the effectiveness of self-help, the character of the self-help process, and relationships with the formal care giving systems. Provides information about and referral to self-help support groups and regional self-help clearinghouses. Conducts media outreach, provides speakers, and publishes manuals, training materials, monographs and policy papers. (National Self-Help Clearinghouse, 2008)

Mutual aid or self-help groups, then, are organizations formed by people with problems for people with problems. Strictly defined, self-help groups do not use professionals to solve their problems; the problem solvers are the problem sufferers, as in the classic example of the 12-step program, Alcoholics Anonymous. Self-help / mutual aid organizations typically deal with two core components of a problem: (1) a difference or condition faced by their members, and (2) a stigma that is associated with the behavior or condition. From the perspective of social deviance we are particularly interested in the ways these groups act to help members cope with their stigma problems, and how they also work to change the public understanding of people with their problems. Part of what self-help / mutual aid groups do is to develop a shared understanding among members about why they formed, which serves to convey important messages to their members about their overall mission.

Sociologists have also sought to understand why they formed in the second half of the twentieth century and they have identified five major reasons. These include: (1) the "growing isolation of individuals stemming from industrialization and urbanization," leading to many feeling alienated and powerless; (2) the "growth of centralized bureaucratic government policy on a variety of social issues," leading to depersonalization and dehumanization and the perception that people have a lack of control over their lives; (3) a desire by individuals for freedom to maintain their anonymity as deviant identities; (4) the effects of accumulated "social protests of the 1950s, 1960s, and 1970s over civil rights, women's issues, and the Vietnam War ... which showed that it was possible to challenge authority with impunity, and that to do so successfully one must organize, engage in civil disobedience, and press for social and political change"; this served to replace beliefs in traditional institutions of the family, church, and state, and laid a foundation for the postmodernist view that progress and traditional power/knowledge structures took more than they gave; and (5) "the growing awareness of the limits of science, and particularly the new helping professions," and the acknowledgment that the professions that had replaced family and church were unable to deal with chronic personal problems of modern society and had abandoned their pretense to do so. This led to a general skepticism about science, and to a lack of trust in its efficacy (Pfuhl and Henry, 1993: 212–13).

Self-help and mutual aid groups form in the context of these macrosocietal trends when there is "dissatisfaction with the status quo, a perception that the existing situation is intolerable, a desire to do something about it, and the vision that this may best be achieved with likeminded others" (Pfuhl and Henry, 1993: 215). Before a group can form it is necessary that stigma sufferers can see that their sense of dissatisfaction can be relieved by sharing their experience with fellow sufferers who are in the same situation as themselves, and that, by coming together, they can collectively work on a solution. Indeed, "by pooling misery, anger and frustration, the groups act as a catalyst for precipitating the relief from knowing one is not alone with the problem and the common interest which leads to a desire to change the situation" (Henry, 1978: 654). Elements that relieve the problem of stigma include: (1) "the common experience of the members . . . the belief . . . that no one is separate, superior, or professional . . . by excluding professionals the separation of stigma sufferers from others within the group is dissolved"; (2) a "shared situation and empathetic understanding that is exemplified by descriptive instances of one's own experience through which another can give relief from knowing you are "not alone with the problem," which "lifts the burden of self-imposed failure, resentment, guilt, and helplessness," and enables one to feel normal in the company of similar others, thereby suspending the public moral meaning of stigma and reducing the stress associated with relations with the non-stigmatized; (3) the value of mutual aid and support on a regular and continuous basis, removing from the problem sufferer the onus of always having to ask for help, and making the problem relatively unremarkable; (4) the "helper-therapy principle" in which people who help others gain most from the exchange because their social status is elevated into a positive role; as a result they obtain validation of their feelings and attitudes, as opposed to the negative experiences that their stigmatized condition has otherwise produced (Pfuhl and Henry, 1993: 216).

Mutual aid groups are "not merely a forum for deconstructing members' problems by coping with practicalities and coping with stigma," but also a "positive process, enabling members to reconstruct a new way of living through project work" (Robinson and Henry, 1977: 94). Project work involves a three-stage process that members of such groups undergo. The first stage involves defining or redefining difficulties in day-to-day coping with problems, and providing information drawn from members' experiences and scientific knowledge about the behavior or conditions and what works to alleviate them: "This information elevates the members into becoming their own authority and simultaneously provides them with the resources to combat the ignorance of others in everyday encounters" (Pfuhl and Henry, 1993: 218). The second stage "involves constructive action towards shared goals based on the philosophy that members learn by doing and are changed by doing . . . projects involve working jointly with others toward a goal that enhances the group for the members" (1993: 218). The third stage occurs when groups begin designing and working on specific projects, such that members go "beyond the group to form a network of friends . . . [which helps] the person give up relying on the all-embracing support of the group, and helps them form new friendship networks in the community" (1993: 218). Indeed, through group work and group talk, members go beyond the group: "Groups emphasize their problem, their projects, their way of doing things, but the real purpose, the hidden agenda, is to transform people" (Robinson and Henry, 1977: 103):

The problem is integrated with life; the treated is the treater and the treatment is to find a new way of living, incorporating the problem into one's everyday experience. This is done by providing a continuous form of care and concern through a network of friendships that itself permeates everyday living and having problems. Thus rather than *living* everyday life and *having* problems self-help group members live their lives *through* their problems. All of the changes in perception about the severity of the problem, the availability of help, the significance of asking for help, of not discontinuing help, require people to change their everyday lives. This is what we mean when we say self-help groups transform people. (1977: 121)

For inner focused groups, who are concentrating on their members' recovery through enabling them to fit better into society, the self-help / mutual aid group provides the community and cognitive structure to enable them to continue. For outer focused groups, the project work involves political action to change the public definition of the deviant behavior. These groups relate the suffering to society's oppression of their situation or condition and seek an "increase in the allocation of resources to the groups' cause, by working for a change in the public's definition of the problem, or by seeking relief through litigation and legislation" (Levine, 1988: 41). As Sagarin and others have pointed out, "the overall aim of many groups is to counter popular beliefs and stereotypical assumptions concerning the causes and consequences of the problematic condition or behavior that is their deviance, and to expose the myths that perpetuate such views" (Pfuhl and Henry, 1993: 230).

In many ways the project work of mutual aid groups is similar to the moral entrepreneur work of rule-makers. Instead of making myths and creating panics, resulting in laws banning behaviors, these groups deconstruct myths, defuse the public's anxiety about the problem or conditions, and seek to legitimate their view by changing law and public policy. For example, stigma management for those suffering from obesity varies from groups like Overeaters Anonymous and WeightWatchers, which are dedicated to changing members' appearance so that they fit into the socially constructed definition of a normal man's or woman's body size, to, in contrast, the National Association to Advance Fat Acceptance (NAAFA), a civil rights organization "engaged in a variety of social and political activities" ranging from "informal parties and organized dances, to speaking at community conferences, to holding protests and conducting write-in campaigns" (Martin 2006: 317). Martin states that "in contrast to avowing or managing shame, NAAFA members contest it . . . 'Change the World, Not Your Body' " is the message of such "fat activism" (2006: 329). He says, "Shame contestation is thus a requisite component of identity politics where the aggrieved attempts to transform themselves by transforming both societal definitions of beauty and human value and the feeling rules that govern fat bodies" (2006: 330).

As Heitzig points out, there are two important consequences of such organized attempts to redefine deviance. One is that of "reverse stigmatization" in which those who reject others are themselves rejected. In this social reordering, "the once-stigmatized now stigmatize the statuses they do not occupy: the white man, rednecks, honkys, male chauvinist pigs, normies, geeks, straights" (Heitzig, 1996: 351). As a vegetarian says in rejecting the stereotype of vegetarians:

> First there are the redneck/macho types who think we're silly, and that we only eat seeds, sprouts and maybe quiche. Then there are health conscious people like joggers or doctors who think we're smart because we only eat healthy foods and never touch things like Coca-Cola, alcohol or Snickers bars. Then there are yuppies who think that we're so good that we're the only ones that are still doing what everyone else was doing in the sixties and early seventies: recycling glass and paper, composting, gardening without chemicals. (Marsh, 1999: 166–7)

The second consequence is the effect on social control of stigmatized statuses:

> The civil rights movements of racial minorities, women, and the elderly have been instrumental in the removal of legally supported stigmatization, as well as the informal perpetuation of many stereotypes . . . pressure from the homosexual movement resulted in the removal of homosexuality from the DSM-IV [the fourth edition of the American Psychiatric Association's *Diagnostic and Statistical Manual of Mental Disorders*]. The organized redefinition of stigma, by the deviants involved, has on occasion removed the formal and medical definitions that long supported the informal stereotypes surrounding stigma. (Heitzig, 1996: 351)

However, before such major societal changes can occur, groups of social deviants have to engage in public relations and media-influencing strategies.

Strategies for redefining deviance

There are several strategies deployed to influence the public. One strategy that is used by deviant groups is to point out that banning the problem makes the situation worse because it forces problem sufferers underground where they are likely to meet and engage in a whole new set of deviant relationships. Also, by banning certain behaviors, additional problems are created. A classic example is that banning marijuana use creates an underground economy of drug sales, which produces violence that draws on policing and court resources.

A second strategy that groups employ is to seek legitimacy for their identity by showing how common their behavior or condition is among the population; how all kinds of people at all different levels of society are subject to it, or suffer from it and its related problems; and how the problem is not restricted to the narrow group depicted in the stereotype. For example, TV ads showing respectable middle-class educated professionals who are HIV-AIDS or genital herpes sufferers dispel the stereotypical myth that, for example, herpes suffers are "people who had multiple partners who . . . went to the bars" (Lee and Craft, 2006: 296). An extension of this tactic is getting endorsements for the group's cause from prestigious and respected members of the community, such as NORML's "use of an Advisory Board on which it lists prominent physicians, attorneys, educators and religious personalities."

To be successful at any of these attempts to redefine the problems and negate the stigma, groups need to master communication and the media. As Altheide (2002; 2007) has argued, deviance and the entertainment and news media are inextricably linked, and it is through the media and popular culture that people learn cultural stereotypes about deviance. Through the media, "Audiences learn to play with deviance by, on the one hand, sharing in stereotypes, being repulsed by certain conduct, and cheering on authorities who seek to eliminate deviance, while, on the other hand, celebrating deviance for its innovations and resistance to convention, and in many instances emulating deviant lifestyles" (Altheide, 2007: 1107). However, he points out that the media does not just passively transmit information about deviance to audiences: rather, "the mass media increasingly help shape the definitions and perceptions about deviance and social order" (2007: 1107). The very fact that the entertainment-oriented mass media are communicating images of deviance "also provides an opportunity for organized spokespersons associated with deviant behavior to express themselves and offer counter claims about their activities, their meanings, and, quite often, their humanity" (2007: 1109).

Personal accounts of problems suffered, depths of self-esteem reached, and ability to rise above them are a mainstay of these organizations. The ability to communicate one's own recovery directly is important. Whereas this information used to be communicated through personal appearances of members to new members, and through written brochures and pamphlets, increasingly this information and video clips are made available on numerous websites devoted to the aims of the organization, as well as through numerous web-based "blogs," and even podcasts.

The presence of the web has not, however, diminished the role of the media in providing coverage, immediacy, and legitimation for groups seeking to transform stigmatizing labels. In this process, it is valuable to have relations with journalists through whom story ideas, promoting the organization's issues, can be channeled. Some groups dedicate, as a project, members who have specific roles in handling media enquiries, interviews, and public relations; other groups have a "press room" on their website. Organizations will also stage events in order to attract media attention. Whatever way groups obtain media coverage of their cause, the framing of message content is important if it is to effectively resonate with the public to change their view of the stigmatized condition. The change is achieved in part by drawing on scientific findings, in part by showing that the whole person is more than that captured by the stereotype, and in part by replacing existing terms that describe the behavior or condition with new words and phrases that carry new meaning that the group desires to impart to the public. This also serves to change members' consciousness. For example a major shift has occurred in many groups who have adopted the phrase "people with" a behavior or condition rather than having the condition define the person. So, instead of talking about "the disabled," groups have changed the public discourse to "people with disabilities." Instead of HIV/AIDS sufferers, it is "people with HIV/AIDS." Instead of anorexics or bulimics, it is "people with anorexia, or bulimia." Consider this advisory from the Resource Center for Independent Living (RCIL):

> Positive language empowers. When writing or speaking about people with disabilities, it is important to put the person first. With any disability, avoid negative, disempowering words, like "victim" or "sufferer." Say "person with AIDS" instead of "AIDS victim" or "person who suffers from AIDS." Group designations such as "the blind," "the retarded" or "the disabled" are inappropriate because they do not reflect the individuality, equality or dignity of people with disabilities. Say "wheelchair user," rather than "confined to a wheelchair" or "wheelchair bound." The wheelchair is what enables the person to get around and participate in society – it's liberating, not confining. (RCIL, 2008)

Vegetarians, for example, will correct those who describe them as "not eating meat" by redefining themselves as "not killing animals" (Marsh, 1999: 168). Changing the common use of discourse and substituting it with "replacement discourse" is critical in making not only social change but also institutional and political change.

Just as it was with rule-makers and rule-creators, whom we earlier called "moral entrepreneurs," making changes in the public policy through enacting laws is often a major objective of groups of social deviants seeking to change the public's view of their stigmatized behavior or condition. Disabilities groups made major reforms that prevented discrimination against people with disabilities that culminated in 1990 with The Americans with Disabilities Act. NORML, which has had considerable success in decriminalizing the laws and stereotyping of marijuana users, continues to make progress towards legalizing its use. A look at NORML's website reveals that it is engaged in direct political action, has a Political Action Committee (PAC) through which it can lobby politicians and officeholders, and uses podcasts and video clips of important political speeches and statements. It contains a report card summarizing what politicians have done, rather than said, about marijuana, and includes extracts of leading politicians' stated policy on drugs in general and marijuana in particular. NORML also has an "in the media" section that features its members' appearances in the media. Its webpage, "A Voice for Responsible Marijuana Smokers," is illustrative:

> Since its founding in 1970, NORML has provided a voice in the public policy debate for those Americans who oppose marijuana prohibition and favor an end to the practice of arresting marijuana smokers. A nonprofit public-interest advocacy group, NORML represents the interests of the tens of millions of Americans who smoke marijuana responsibly . . . During the 1970s, NORML led the successful efforts to decriminalize minor marijuana offenses in 11 states and significantly lower marijuana penalties in all others. Today NORML continues to lead the fight to reform state and federal marijuana laws, whether by voter initiative or through the elected legislatures. NORML serves as an informational resource to the national media on marijuana-related stories, providing a perspective to offset the anti-marijuana propaganda from the government; lobbies state and federal legislators in support of reform legislation; publishes a regular newsletter; hosts, along with the NORML Foundation, an informative web site and an annual conference; and serves as the umbrella group for a national network of citizen-activists committed to ending marijuana prohibition and legalizing marijuana. Our sister organization, the NORML Foundation sponsors public advertising campaigns to better educate the public about marijuana and alternatives to current marijuana policy; provides legal assistance and support to victims of the current laws; and undertakes relevant research. The oldest and largest marijuana legalization organization in the country, NORML maintains a professional staff in Washington, DC, headed by Executive Director Allen St. Pierre, and a network of volunteer state and local NORML Chapters across the country. (NORML, 2008)

Clearly the actions of NORML are illustrative of the extent to which organizations formed by and for deviants engage in power politics over the competition for interests – what Edwin Schur (1980) described as "stigma contests":

> In these continuing struggles over competing social definitions, it is relative, rather than absolute power that counts most . . . Deviance-defining is not a static event but a continuous and changing process. This is so because . . . it is a way of characterizing and reacting, exhibited by individuals and groups whose interests and favored values, and their ability to impose them, vary greatly and in many instances change over time . . . the distribution of power among persons and groups crucially shapes deviance outcomes. To study stigma contests or deviance struggles is, then, to study the sources and uses of power. (1980: 8, 66)

Ultimately, the aim of all of these counter political strategies, whether designed to help their members fit into the existing society, or to transform the society to accept their deviance in what some have referred to as the "sociology of acceptance" (Bogdan and Taylor, 1987), is to normalize the relations between the deviant and society. Groups of organized deviants want their members' difference to be accepted as normal.

Becoming normal

In order for someone designated with the stigma of a "deviant" label to become normal, they and others have to ultimately recognize what "normal" means. As I stated at the outset, normality is not the complete absence of deviance; that itself would be deviant. It is, rather, the presence of deviance as one of a range of behavioral options, or one of a range of non-stigmatized, morally neutral differences. Occasionally, normal identities are free to choose deviance without serious moral implications for self or others. Its choosing does not bring about any questioning of the actor's identity, nor does it raise the specter of some real deviant identity lurking beneath the surface should the behavior be exposed. Being normal means being free to choose deviance without serious consequences and not choosing it most of the time. But how can someone who has suffered serious challenge to their identity resume their former position of normality? Clearly, forming relations of mutual support with fellow deviants does not return an actor to normalcy, because most of those who have not been stigmatized do not have relations with others based solely on their participation in a morally condemned or stigmatized behavior. While self-help groups are a transition to normality, they are not its final resting place. This lies in the ability of those stigmatized to select, from all those with whom they formerly had relations, only those who maintain an open-minded, supportive relationship. It also requires that new relations be formed such that interaction of the present begins to construct a new biography, which eventually builds to form its own history. All of this may require a change of location; it certainly requires sufficient confidence to award oneself the right to be normal. In short, it requires that the deviant who seriously does not want to be so cast ceases to invest in that which gives pain and starts again, building a new life and a new identity.

Conclusion: what can studying social deviance do for you?

To answer this question, it is important to realize what students of social deviance study and why. Sociologist Erich Goode captures the spirit of why studying deviance is important when he reflects on his own decades-long interest in the subject:

> I'm interested in how definitions of right and wrong are established and maintained, how collectivities in every society struggle, over notions of what is to be demarcated as acceptable and unacceptable behavior, beliefs, and even physical traits; what and who will be stigmatized; what and who will be honored and respected, what and who will be ignored, accepted, tolerated and condoned. What and who will be regarded as *emblematic* of society as a whole, and what and who will be relegated to the margins, emblematic only of the society's periphery – not entirely respectable, exemplary, or reputable . . . as I see it, the central idea in the sociology of deviance is that definitions of right and wrong do not drop from the skies. They are not preordained. They are humanly *produced*, *constructed* as a result of clashes of ideologies, interests – economic, social, cultural, political – the outcome of struggles between and among categories in the society, each vying for dominance, or at least acceptance, of the views and behaviors that categorize them as a social entity. (Goode, 2009: 566)

As people, we are each different. Each of us is someone to take notice of, and we are, in some important senses, capable of shaping the world we live in. But we also see that, even when we strive to be different, our interaction with others binds us to conform. That we don't conform to wider societal morality and law is no evidence that we don't conform, for our very joining with others who share our conventional or deviant activity is an indication of the force of those around us. We declare independence when we say that we don't care what others think, but we reveal our vulnerability in our sensitivity to what friends and co-deviants think. We are individuals but we are also social beings. We might be able to tilt the balance, but it is the truly extreme social deviant who is unaffected by aspects of both these internal and external forces.

Because of the contested terrain that Goode refers to as the politics of deviance, what we learn from the study of deviance will depend in part on our own values and interests. It will also depend on how far we are able to suspend our moral judgments in order to appreciate the meanings of those who are doing things we find offensive and objectionable. Without suspending such judgments, it is not possible to obtain the trust of those engaged in often incriminating, sometimes self-deprecating, behaviors that we call "deviance." Without obtaining their trust, it would not be possible to peer inside their social worlds to see what is fundamental in our own. Studying deviance then requires us to look outside ourselves as a means to gaining insight on what we all do on a daily basis.

Ultimately, I believe we must reject the view of those, like Anne Hendershott, or for that matter the Catholic Church, who say that morally relativistic or appreciative explorations of social deviance render us culturally and morally rudderless; that giving every meaning credibility, every identification of difference legitimacy, means that we can ultimately say nothing, and, worse, that we are unable to condemn deviance as bad, evil, or morally wrong. Such a view misses the fundamental point of social deviance: it is not that the difference that is deviant is morally wrong, but that behavior and action that harms others is morally wrong. The irony of social life is that most of what counts as deviance harms no one, although it might "offend" – but that is an entirely different matter.

Social deviance, then, is both a celebration and condemnation of difference. Difference enables us to adapt to changing circumstances. It gives us the possibilities to survive. Conformity is tied to what is. To recognize difference, indeed to appreciate and understand a multiplicity of differences, is both seeing and saying a lot. It is saying that we are not completely bound by the constraints of past structures or current constructions of reality, that our own agency can make a difference, that what you think and what I think matters. That the difference made is one that some, or even many, find offensive should not blind us to the importance of the struggle we all have to make a difference. It should, instead, alert us to the fundamental importance of societal institutions and broader structures to facilitate the means for individual recognition, because it will emerge if we try to suppress it and its emergence may not please us.

Does this exploration of social deviance mean that we cannot make moral judgments? Of course it doesn't. We can make much more informed judgments than those we would have made without the appreciation and understanding of the meanings of those who take part in deviant behavior. To understand the meaning of social deviance and then to weigh that activity in the light of a wider social context is to make a responsible judgment about the activity. To fail to attempt to understand that to which we object is taking the same irresponsible attitude that we find offensive in others. We do not care. Why should they?

So, in studying deviance, it is first necessary to suspend our moral judgment in order to appreciate the phenomenon from the perspective of the other. Doing so requires that we treat deviance as difference and explore the ways that these differences are carved out of the social cloth of everyday life and given significance, imbued with meaning, reacted to by others, and built into social objects, institutional practices, and social processes. To study deviance is to study the social construction of normality. It is to shine a light into what sociologist Peter Berger once called our "reasonably comfortable caves" in order to reveal the graffiti on the walls, the crap on the floor, and our moral nakedness with its attendant vulnerabilities. As students of the sociology of deviance, we are exploring what for sociologist Erving Goffman was the back stage behind the front stage that makes the front stage possible. In this sense, the study of social deviance is the flip side of the study of normality; the study of social deviance is the underside of the study of social order; the study of rule violation is a mirror to the study of conformity. And although we might start out by looking at the strange, peculiar, and different, students soon realize that social deviance is as much in their own lives as it is in the lives of those they study. Indeed, the study of others' social deviance soon reveals the ubiquity of social deviance in social life. A glimpse of the profound interest in things deviant is found in the mass media's obsessive fascination with all things deviant in its "fictional and nonfictional stories about the 'dark side' of society":

> Think about how many people routinely watch television shows like *NYPD Blue*, *The John Walsh Show*, *CSI Miami*, *Law and Order*, *The Sopranos*, and so on. Further, much of North Americans' everyday conversation, regardless of whether it occurs at home, in the workplace, bars, classrooms, at sporting events and so on, includes stories

about friends, relatives, celebrities, athletes, politicians, and others who did the "wrong stuff" ... as well as debates about what is to be done about these "outsiders" behaviors, beliefs, and attitudes. (DeKeseredy, Ellis and Alvi, 2005: 1–2)

But we need not rely on the media alone to provide packaged insights into social deviance. We need simply to look around us at everyday life to see that deviance is in everything we do. Consider this day-in-the-life of a university student and her reflections on social deviance in her everyday life. She entitles the piece "To Be Average Is To Be Deviant":

Deviance is at its core a social construction that is used to maintain social order. Although deviant acts are by definition constructed as that which is outside the norm, deviance (... outside the box of expected and or acceptable behavior) is startlingly normal (defined as commonly occurring and acceptable). Our days are filled with transgressions of varying magnitude, some our own and some those of others.

7:34 a.m. – Wake up late, failure of self regulation. Start to get ready for the day. Rush to shower so that I will still be on time for work because normal, stable people are timely. Flip through channels while making breakfast. Think to myself, "TV is not normal." Get stuck on the infomercials for a little while. Wonder why people in exercise videos are always smiling. Is it normal to smile when you're inflicting pain on yourself? Take steak out of the fridge and throw it into a pan. My mother asks if I'm making the steak for lunch. I tell her that it's for breakfast. She tells me that steak is not a breakfast food, but I tell her not to worry because at college they give us breakfast for dinner sometimes and she just rolls her eyes and asks me if I'm trying to make her feel bad and if this is what she's paying for.

8:00 a.m. Check email. Find a forward from my dad in inbox. Think about how much funnier the dance is when Shane Mercado does it than when Beyonce does it. Kind of feel like I'm not supposed to laugh because I know that the performance is funny mostly because it undermines normative heterosexuality and as a progressive thinker I should take the project of weakening the heteronormative matrix seriously, but that said I still find the video hilarious. Check *Facebook*. Procrastinate on *Youtube* for a while and check out the new virtual symphony orchestra that is being formed. Tell me the on-line conducting video is not abnormal. Stumble onto a dance show video. Am slightly disturbed: a) by how good these kids are, b) by how crazy show kid culture is, but mostly by c) how sexual the dance that these kids are doing seems. Watch some "Imaginary Bitches." Decide to do productive things with my life.

The normals draw lines for the population to follow. As a society we pay homage to these lines and experience anxiety when they are crossed. We hold the categories that we have created as holy and respect them as naturally occurring phenomena that have always been drawn in stone as a guide for behavior. We act as if race and social class created themselves as organizational blocks of what people should expect in life. We act as if child brides were never a Western phenomenon and as if Ashton and Demi, now that they have been validated by the media, are the first couple to ever have such a large age gap in their relationship. We pretend that on the day that a person turns twenty-one their brain is suddenly extremely less susceptible to the damages of alcohol on the brain and significantly more mature to make decisions about drinking.

9:00 a.m. Get to the gym. Put my ipod on and get on elliptical machine. Read some Catcher in the Rye while on the elliptical. Secretly think I am Holden Caufield at heart.

I would argue that if we had never invented deviance secrets wouldn't exist and if we think about how silly most secrets are our continual need to label people as deviant seems a bit silly too. A secret is just a secret because someone decided that whatever is being kept secret is unacceptable public behavior or knowledge. What's so different between secrets and deviance?

10:30 a.m. Walk back from the gym. Call mom. Ask again about taking time off from school. She tells me that time off is only for people who are screwing up or get pregnant or go crazy or . . . I drop the argument.

I always drop the argument, partly because even though I think that the American model of formal education leads to widespread and excessive burn out which I often experience, college isn't that bad and I have been conditioned to be here for four years. Besides I would much rather be controlled through the apparatuses of civil society than those of the state. The concept of the gap-year (a year taken off between high-school and college – common in Europe and becomingly increasingly popular in certain segments of the American population) might be one of the most interesting trends in contemporary youth culture to look at the intersection of Marxian theories of deviance and the idea of subjectivities. There are people for whom the subjectivity of time off before college weighs equally heavy with the subjectivity of college as the natural way for a person to spend their next four years after high school. Of course there are a range of other possibilities such as not attending college at all, attending a two year college, attending college part-time while working, and taking time off during college. Each of these options is marked by race, class, gender, nationality, geography, and other increasingly multitudinous social factors. These factors combine to create different potential responses along a continuum of stigma and acceptance for the same decision made by different people. Whether they admit it or not there is way in which as a black female I am already the discredited so my parents worry about me playing with the things that make me the discreditable. Maybe I worry about it too, but not as much.

11:00 a.m. Psychology class. Praise the American Psychiatric Association a little for perfecting social control through the DSM.

12:15 p.m. Lunch. Absolutely hate lunch at this time because it's so crowded. It makes me feel institutionalized.

1:30 p.m. Deviance and Social Order class. Professor is being deviant again – you know, flexible and understanding. Reasonable. Okay, professors aren't bad in general.

2:45 p.m. Lit Theory class. All of the theorists that we are reading were considered deviant in their times. I'm surprised that more of them weren't hung or put on house arrest or something. Jaywalk on my way back to my dorm. A driver angrily shakes his hand at me.

Deviance is always relative. What is acceptable in one era is reprehensible in another. What is okay in the city is punishable on the farm.

4:30 p.m. Go back to room. Check in with friends. Turn on computer. Check email and *Facebook*. Watch funny video on the homepage of *Slate Magazine*, a respectable, but entertaining on-line magazine. Do some homework. Think about the fact that paying a lot of money for the privilege of working really hard to the end of working really hard for the rest of your life is unnatural.

6:00 p.m. Dinner. Partake in the Middlebury College two-bowl dinner ritual: Make dinner i.e. a salad and throw on some dressing and use the second bowl to shake it. I like doing it because I think it looks cool like when someone makes me a tossed salad at a deli and it spreads the dressing well. My friends give me the look. I remind them that I'm going to get other food too.

7:00 p.m. Do some more homework. Feel a little bit depressed; wonder if I need Zoloft.

10:00 p.m. Hang out with friends. Spike some cider, because drinking on week-nights is more acceptable in college and during certain parts of the year. We call it a holiday party so it's okay. Watch some Mean Girls and The Secret Diary of a Call Girl. Someone brings up pole dancing . . . wish the classes were cheaper.

The entertainment industry should praise daily the constructions of normalcy and deviance. Most entertainment especially in terms of movies and television are based on deviance in that they either draw strength from their universality, that is the way in which everyone can relate and is the same because the experience depicted is expected; normal, or they draw off of the attraction to that which falls somewhere other than on the list of what is normal, accepted, or expected; deviant. Even in terms of activities people always want to try things that seem risqué, whether it's bungee jumping or pole dancing both of which have become increasingly popular over the years. In the case of pole dancing the activity's transformation from something meant only for strippers to something for average women to do for exercise and to feel sexy reads as similar to the re-appropriation of negative words that has always been common with disenfranchised groups.

1:00 a.m. Sleep

We live through our transgressions. In my eyes life is most invigorating when we're breaking the rules. I don't care what you call it – deviant behavior, secrets or crime – we all deviate. Picking up where Erickson left off, I would claim that deviance is necessary not only for the maintenance of the society, but also the enrichment of the individual. If establishing laws is a way for the "authorities" in a society to claim phallic power for themselves, purposeful deviance is an assertion of agency and a claim to phallic power on an individual level. Of course not all deviance is planned since deviance only becomes deviance once enough people with power label it as such, but the existence of "deviance" is what allows us to live in a world in which we're not all like-minded cyborgs. (Nesbeth, 2008: reproduced with permission.)

In the first chapter of this book I pointed out that a few sociologists believed that the study of deviance is dead. Most others would agree with Erich Goode that it is very much alive. If you don't believe that, just go out, look around and you'll observe life's rich tapestry of deviant behavior. In doing so, develop your own deviant imagination and appreciation for the social processes that "invigorate" and "enrich" us all.

References

Adler, Patricia A., and Peter Adler, eds. 2006. *Constructions of Deviance: Social Power, Context and Interaction.* 5th edn. Belmont, CA: Thompson Wadsworth.

Altheide, David L. 2002. *Creating Fear: News and the Construction of Crisis.* Hawthorn, NY: Aldine de Gruyter.

2007. "The media and Deviance," pp. 1107–10 in *The Blackwell Encyclopedia of Sociology*, vol. III. Ed. G. Ritzer. Oxford: Blackwell Publishing.

Becker, Howard. 1963. *Outsiders: Studies in the Sociology of Deviance.* New York: Free Press.

Boal, Mark. 2008. "Everyone Will Remember Me as Some Sort of Monster." *Rolling Stone*, 1059 (August 21): 73–80.

Bogdan, Robert, and S. Taylor. 1987. "Toward a Sociology of Acceptance: The Other Side of a Study of Deviance." *Social Policy*, 18: 34–9.

Boles, David. 1997. "Cultural Differences v Social Deviancy." *Go Inside.* http://goinside.com/97/5/deviancy.html.

Bower, Bruce. 1996. "Fighting Stereotype Stigma: Studies Chart Accuracy, Usefulness of Inferences about Social Groups." *Science News*, 149 (June 29): 408.

Bowlby, John. 1988. *A Secure Base: Clinical Applications of Attachment Theory.* London: Routledge.

Box, Steven. 1981. *Deviance, Reality and Society.* New York: Holt, Rinehart and Winston.

Bradley, Bud. 1999. "Fraternity Drinking," pp. 93–7 in *Degrees of Deviance: Student Accounts of Their Deviant Behavior.* Ed. S. Henry and R. Eaton. Salem, WI: Sheffield Publishing Company.

Brekhus, Wayne. 1998. "A Sociology of the Unmarked: Redirecting our Focus." *Sociological Theory*, 16.1: 36.

2000. "A Mundane Manifesto." *Journal of Mundane Behavior.* www. mundanebehavior.org/issues/v1n1/brekhus.htm (accessed January 15, 2009).

Brown, Patricia Leigh. 1988. "Troubled Millions Heed the Call of Self-help Groups." *New York Times,* July 16. http://query.nytimes.com/gst/fullpage.html? res=940DE2D71F38F935A25754C0A96E948260 (accessed July 15, 2008).

Clark, Winston. 1999. "Athletes' Little Helpers," pp. 82–5 in *Degrees of Deviance: Student Accounts of Their Deviant Behavior.* Ed. S. Henry and R. Eaton. Salem, WI: Sheffield Publishing Company.

Cohen, Stanley. 1972. *Folk Devils and Moral Panics: The Creation of Mods and Rockers.* New York: St. Martin's Press.

Comuzzie, Anthony G., and David B. Allison. 1998. "The Search for Human Obesity Genes." *Science,* 280: 1374–7.

Cooley, Charles Horton. 1902. *Human Nature and the Social Order.* New York: Charles Scribner's and Sons.

Counts, Dorothy E., and David R. Counts. 1991. "'People Who Act like Dogs': Adultery and Deviance in a Melanesian Community." *Anthropologica,* 33.1–2: 99–110.

Cressey, Donald R. 1953. *Other People's Money.* Glencoe, IL: Free Press.

1970. "The Respectable Criminal," pp. 105–16 in *Modern Criminals.* Ed. James Short. New York: Transaction-Aldine.

Crocker, Jennifer, Brenda Major, and C. Steele. 1998. "Social Stigma," pp. 504–53 in *Handbook of Social Psychology.* 4th edn. Ed. D. T. Gilbert, S. T. Fiske, and G. Lindzey. Boston: McGraw-Hill.

DeKeseredy, Walter S., Desmond Ellis, and Shahid Alvi. 2005. *Deviance and Crime: Theory, Research and Policy.* 3rd edn. Cincinnati, OH: Anderson Publishing / LexisNexis.

de Young, Mary. 1997. "The Devil Goes to Day Care: McMartin and the Making of a Moral Panic." *Journal of American Culture,* 20: 19–26.

2006. "Moral Panics: The Case of Satanic Day Care Centers," pp. 162–70 in *Constructions of Deviance: Social Power, Context and Interaction.* 5th edn. Ed. P. A. Adler and P. Adler. Belmont, CA: Thompson Wadsworth.

Dotter, Daniel L. 2004. *Creating Deviance: An Interactionist Approach.* New York: Rowman Altamira.

Dovidio, John F., Brenda Major, and Jennifer Crocker. 2000. "Stigma: Introduction and Overview," pp. 1–28 in *The Social Psychology of Stigma.* Ed. T.F Heatherton, R. E. Kleck, M. R. Hebl, and J. G. Hull. New York: The Guilford Press.

Eakin, Emily. 2000. "The Mundane Seeks Equal Time With the Weird and the Deviant," *New York Times.* www.mundanebehavior.org/press/nytimes_arts. htm (accessed February 1, 2009).

Ellis, Lee, and Anthony Walsh. 1997. "Gene-Based Evolutionary Theories in Criminology." *Criminology,* 35: 229–76.

Fairchild, Carol. 1999. "Compliment of the Hospital," pp. 62–4 in *Degrees of Deviance: Student Accounts of Their Deviant Behavior.* Ed. S. Henry and R. Eaton. Salem, WI: Sheffield Publishing Company.

Fishbein, Diana H. 1998. "Biological Perspectives in Criminology," pp. 92–109 in *The Criminology Theory Reader*. Ed. S. Henry and W. Einstadter. New York: New York University Press.

Frost, Janet. 1999. "Affairs," pp. 30–2, in *Degrees of Deviance: Student Accounts of Their Deviant Behavior*. Ed. S. Henry and R. Eaton. Salem, WI: Sheffield Publishing Company.

Furlong, Michael J., Bonita Sharma, and Sujin Sabrina Rhee. 2000. "Defining School Violence Victory Subtypes: A Step Toward Adapting Prevention and Intervention Programs to Match Student Needs," pp. 67–87, in *Violence in American Schools: A Practical Guide for Counselors*. Ed. D. S. Sandhu and C. B. Aspy. Alexandria, VA: American Counseling Association.

Gabor, Thomas. 1994. *Everyone's Doing It!* Toronto: University of Toronto.

Goffman, Erving. 1959. *The Presentation of Self in Everyday Life*. Harmondsworth: Penguin.

1963. *Stigma, Notes on the Management of Spoiled Identity*. Englewood Cliffs, NJ: Prentice Hall.

1971. *Relations in Public*. Harmondsworth: Penguin.

Good, Tyrone. 1999. "Cyberporn," pp. 40–4 in *Degrees of Deviance: Student Accounts of Their Deviant Behavior*. Ed. S. Henry and R. Eaton. Salem, WI: Sheffield Publishing Company.

Goode, Erich. 2000. *Paranormal Beliefs: A Sociological Introduction*. Prospect Heights, IL: Waveland Press.

2002. "Does the Death of the Sociology of Deviance Claim Make Sense?" *American Sociologist*, 33: 116–28.

2004. "Is the Sociology of Deviance Still Relevant?" *American Sociologist*, 35.4: 46–57.

2007. "Deviance," pp. 1075–82 in *The Blackwell Encyclopedia of Sociology*, vol. III. Ed. George Ritzer. Oxford: Blackwell Publishing.

2009. "The Relevance of the Sociology of Deviance," pp. 565–73 in *Constructions of Deviance: Social Power, Context and Interaction*. 6th edn. Ed. Patricia A. Adler and Peter Adler. Belmont, CA: Thompson Wadsworth.

Goode, Erich, and Norman Ben-Yehuda. 1994. *Moral Panics: The Social Construction of Deviance*. Cambridge: Blackwell.

Goode, Erich, and D. Angus Vail. 2007. *Extreme Deviance*. Thousand Oaks, CA: Pine Forge Press.

Gottfredson, Michael F., and Travis Hirschi. 1990. *A General Theory of Crime*. Stanford: Stanford University Press.

Graham, Paul. 2003. "Why Nerds are Unpopular." www.paulgraham.com/nerds.html (accessed July 15, 2008).

Gusfield, Joseph R. 1963. *Symbolic Crusade*. Urbana, IL: University of Illinois Press.

Hagan, John. 1977. *The Disreputable Pleasures*. Toronto: McGraw-Hill Ryerson.

1985. *Modern Criminology: Crime, Criminal Behavior and Its Control*. New York: McGraw-Hill.

Hanson, F. Allan. 2000. "Where Have All the Abnormal People Gone?" *The Humanist*, 60.2 (March): 29–32.

Heckert, Alex, and Druann Maria Heckert. 2002. "A New Typology of Deviance: Integrating Normative and Reactivist Definitions of Deviance." *Deviant Behavior: An Interdisciplinary Journal,* 23: 449–79.

2004. "Using an Integrated Typology of Deviance to Analyze Ten Common Norms of the U.S. Middle Class." *The Sociological Quarterly,* 45.2: 209–28.

Heckert, Druann. 1998. "Positive Deviance: A Classificatory Model." *Free Inquiry in Creative Sociology,* 26: 23–30.

Heimer, Karen, and Ross L. Matsueda. 1994. "Role-taking, Role Commitment, and Delinquency: A Theory of Differential Social Control." *American Sociological Review,* 59: 365–90.

Heitzig, Nancy A. 1996. *Deviance: Rule Makers and Rule Breakers.* Minneapolis / St. Paul, MN: West Publishing.

Hendershott, Anne. 2002. *The Politics of Deviance.* San Francisco, CA: Encounter.

Henry, Stuart. 1978. "The Dangers of Self-help Groups." *New Society,* 44: 654–6.

Henry, Stuart, and Roger Eaton, eds. 1999. *Degrees of Deviance: Student Accounts of Their Deviant Behavior.* Salem, WI: Sheffield Publishing Company.

Hirschi, Travis. 1969. *The Causes of Delinquency.* Berkeley, CA: University of California Press.

Hirschi, Travis, and Michael R. Gottfredson. 2001. "Self-Control Theory," pp. 81–96 in *Explaining Criminals and Crime.* Ed. R. Paternoster and R. Bachman. Los Angeles: Roxbury Press.

Katz, Alfred H. 1981. "Self-Help and Mutual Aid: An Emerging Social Movement? *Annual Review of Sociology,* 7: 129–55.

Katz, Alfred H., and Eugene I. Bender. 1976. *The Strength In Us: Self-Help Groups in the Modern World.* New York: Franklin Watts.

King, Susan. 1999. "New Wave Culture," pp. 158–61 in *Degrees of Deviance: Student Accounts of Their Deviant Behavior.* Ed. S. Henry and R. Eaton. Salem, WI: Sheffield Publishing Company.

Klockars, Carl B. 1974. *The Professional Fence.* New York: Free Press.

Lanier, Mark, and Stuart Henry. 2004 [1998]. *Essential Criminology.* 2nd edn. Boulder, CO: Westview Press.

Larkin, Ralph W. 2007. *Comprehending Columbine.* Philadelphia: Temple University Press.

Lee, James Daniel, and Elizabeth A. Craft. 2006. "Protecting One's Self from a Stigmatized Disease," pp. 293–303 in *Constructions of Deviance: Social Power, Context and Interaction.* 5th edn. Ed. P. A. Adler and P. Adler. Belmont, CA: Thompson Wadsworth.

Lemert, Edwin M. 1967. *Human Deviance, Social Problems and Social Control.* Englewood Cliffs, NJ: Prentice-Hall.

Levine, Murray. 1988. "How Self-Help Works." *Social Policy,* 18 (summer): 39–43.

Liazos, Alexander. 1972. "The Poverty of the Sociology of Deviance: Nuts, Sluts, and Perverts." *Social Problems,* 20: 103–20.

Lockhart, Lisa. 1999. "Sidework," pp. 54–7 in *Degrees of Deviance: Student Accounts of Their Deviant Behavior*. Ed. S. Henry and R. Eaton. Salem, WI: Sheffield Publishing Company.

Lockwood, Daniel. 1997. *Violence Among Middle School and High School Students: An Analysis and Implications for Prevention*. Washington, DC: US Department of Justice, Office of Justice Programs, National Institute of Justice.

Louganis, Greg (with Eric Marcus). 1995. *Breaking the Surface*. New York: Random House.

Malone, Scott. 1999. "Securing the Shopping Mall," pp. 65–8 in *Degrees of Deviance: Student Accounts of Their Deviant Behavior*. Ed. S. Henry and R. Eaton. Salem, WI: Sheffield Publishing Company.

Marsh, Helen. 1999. "Vegetarianism," pp. 164–8, in *Degrees of Deviance: Student Accounts of Their Deviant Behavior*. Ed. S. Henry and R. Eaton. Salem, WI: Sheffield Publishing Company.

Martin, Daniel D. 2006. "Collective Stigma Management and Shame: Avowal, Management, and Contestation," pp. 315–33 in *Constructions of Deviance: Social Power, Context and Interaction*. 5th edn. Ed. P. A. Adler and P. Adler. Belmont, CA: Thompson Wadsworth.

Maruna, Shadd, and Heith Copes. 2004. "Excuses, Excuses: What Have We Learned from Five Decades of Neutralization Research?" pp. 1–100 in *Crime and Justice*, vol. XXXII: *A Review of Research*. Ed. Michael Tonry. Chicago: University of Chicago Press.

Matsueda, Ross L. 1992. "Reflected Appraisals, Parental Labeling and Delinquency: Specifying an Interactionist Theory." *American Journal of Sociology*, 97: 1577–611.

2001. "Labeling Theory: Historical Roots, Implications and Recent Developments," pp. 223–41 in *Explaining Criminals and Crime*. Ed. Raymond Paternoster and Ronet Bachman. Los Angeles: Roxbury Press.

Matza, David. 1964. *Delinquency and Drift*. New York: John Wiley & Sons.

Michaels, Jay. 1999. "Athletes on Steroids," pp. 79–82 in *Degrees of Deviance: Student Accounts of Their Deviant Behavior*. Ed. S. Henry and R. Eaton. Salem, WI: Sheffield Publishing Company.

Miller, Carol T., and Brenda Major. 2000. "Coping with Stigma and Prejudice," pp. 243–72 in *The Social Psychology of Stigma*. Ed. T. F. Heatherton, R. E. Kleck, M. R. Hebl, and J. G. Hull. New York: The Guilford Press.

Miller, Linda. 1999. "Waiting for Tips," pp. 47–9 in *Degrees of Deviance: Student Accounts of Their Deviant Behavior*. Ed. S. Henry and R. Eaton. Salem, WI: Sheffield Publishing Company.

Mills, Martin. 2001. *Challenging Violence in Schools: An Issue of Masculinities*. Philadelphia: Open University Press.

Moss, Louis. 1999. "Guns and Bottle Rockets," pp. 134–6 in *Degrees of Deviance: Student Accounts of Their Deviant Behavior*. Ed. S. Henry and R. Eaton. Salem, WI: Sheffield Publishing Company.

National Self-Help Clearinghouse. 2004. www.selfhelpweb.org/ (accessed August 31, 2008).

Nesbeth, Megan. 2008. "To Be Average Is To Be Deviant." http://mnesbeth. wordpress.com/ (accessed December 20, 2008).

Newman, Katherine S., Cybelle Fox, David J. Harding, Jal Mehta, and Wendy Roth. 2004. *Rampage: The Social Roots of School Shootings.* New York: Basic Books.

NJ and American Self-help Clearinghouse. 2006. www.selfhelpgroups.org/ (accessed August 30, 2008).

NORML. 2008. "A Voice for Responsible Marijuana Smokers." http://norml. org/index.cfm?Group_ID=5493 (accessed August 30, 2008).

North, Tom. 1999. "Theft of Military Equipment," pp. 68–70 in *Degrees of Deviance: Student Accounts of Their Deviant Behavior.* Ed. S. Henry and R. Eaton. Salem, WI: Sheffield Publishing Company.

Page, Andy. 1999. "Parking Lot Parties," pp. 100–2 in *Degrees of Deviance: Student Accounts of Their Deviant Behavior.* Ed. S. Henry and R. Eaton. Salem, WI: Sheffield Publishing Company.

Park, Kristin. 2006. "Stigma Management among the Voluntary Childless," pp. 304–14 in *Constructions of Deviance: Social Power, Context and Interaction.* 5th edn. Ed. P. A. Adler and P. Adler. Belmont, CA: Thompson Wadsworth.

Parker, Richard, and Peter Aggleton. 2002. *HIV/AIDS-related Stigma and Discrimination: A Conceptual Framework and an Agenda for Action.* New York: The Population Council, Inc.

Perrin, Robin D. 2007. "Deviant Beliefs / Cognitive Deviance," pp. 1140–1 in *The Blackwell Encyclopedia of Sociology,* vol. III. Ed. G. Ritzer. Oxford: Blackwell Publishing.

Pershing, Jana L. 2003. "To Snitch or Not to Snitch? Applying the Concept of Neutralization Techniques to the Enforcement of Occupational Misconduct." *Sociological Perspectives,* 46.2 (Summer): 149–78.

Pfuhl, Erdwin H., and Stuart Henry. 1993. *The Deviance Process.* 3rd edn. New York: Aldine de Gruyter.

Pogue, David. 2007. "The Generational Divide in Copyright Morality." *New York Times,* December 20. www.nytimes.com/2007/12/20/technology/ personaltech/20pogue-email.html (accessed August 30, 2008).

Reasononline. 2001. "Lighten Up, America! Do Fat People Belong in Public Parks?" (December 25). www.reason.com/news/show/35948.html (accessed January 25, 2009).

RCIL. 2008 [2004]. "Fact Sheet: Tips for Communicating with and about People with Disabilities." Utica, NY: Resource Center for Independent Living. www. rcil.com/PressRoom/factsheet.html (accessed August 30, 2008).

Riessman, Frank. 1965. "The Helper-Therapy Principle." *Social Work,* 10: 27–32.

Robinson, David, and Stuart Henry. 1977. *Self-help and Health: Mutual Aid for Modern Problems.* Oxford: Martin Robertson.

Rook, Katie, and Amy Smithers. 2007. "Muslim Girls Can Play Cultural Chameleons." *National Post,* December 11. www.nationalpost.com/todays_ paper/story.html?id=161350 (accessed January 18, 2009).

Rosenhan, D. L. 1995. "Being Sane in Insane Places," pp. 287–96 in Ed. Nancy J. Herman. *Deviance: A Symbolic Interactionist Approach.* New York: General Hall.

Sagarin, Edward. 1969. *Odd Man In: Societies of Deviants in America*. Chicago: Quadrangle Books.

San Diego Alcohol Policy Panel. 2009. "San Diego Beaches Alcohol-Free." http://alcoholpolicypanel.org/sdcappblog/?p=41 (accessed April 11, 2009).

Scapegoat Society. 2003. "Scapegoating Research and Remedies." www.scapegoat.demon.co.uk (accessed April 18, 2009).

Schur, Edwin. M. 1980. *The Politics of Deviance: Stigma Contests and the Uses of Power*. Englewood Cliffs, NJ: Prentice Hall.

Shaw, Karen. 1999. "Sex, Drugs and Dancing Girls," pp. 36–40 in *Degrees of Deviance: Student Accounts of Their Deviant Behavior*. Ed. S. Henry and R. Eaton. Salem, WI: Sheffield Publishing Company.

Shea, Jennifer. 2007. *Adultery among Deployed Naval Military Officers: An Application of Neutralization Theory*. Masters thesis. San Diego State University.

Simon, David R. 2008. *Elite Deviance*. 9th edn. Boston: Allyn & Bacon.

SIRC. 2004. *Smells Like Teen Spirit: Talking Not Taking in the Teenage Music Tribe*. Oxford: Social Issues Research Center. www.sirc.org/publik/frank.pdf.

Smart, Laura, and Daniel M. Wegner. 2000. "The Hidden Costs of Hidden Stigma," pp. 220–42 in *The Social Psychology of Stigma*. Ed. T. F Heatherton, R. E. Kleck, M. R. Hebl, and J. G. Hull. New York: The Guilford Press.

SmokeFree Illinois. 2008. "SmokeFree Illinois: Frequently Asked Questions." www.smokefreeillinois.org/impres/FAQ.pdf.

Spreitzer, Gretchen M., and Scott Sonenshein. 2004. "Toward the Construct Definition of Positive Deviance." *American Behavioral Scientist*, 47.6: 828–47.

Stafford, Gina. 1999. "Pasta Anyone?" pp. 52–4 in *Degrees of Deviance: Student Accounts of Their Deviant Behavior*. Ed. S. Henry and R. Eaton. Salem, WI: Sheffield Publishing Company.

Sumner, Colin. 1994. *The Sociology of Deviance: An Obituary*. Buckingham: Open University Press.

2006. "Deviance," pp. 126–7 in *The Sage Dictionary of Criminology*. 2nd edn. Ed. E. McLaughlin and J. Muncie. London: Sage.

Surette, Ray. 1998. *Media, Crime and Criminal Justice: Images and Realities*. 2nd edn. Belmont, CA: West/Wadsworth.

Targetofopportunity.com. 2009. http://targetofopportunity.com (accessed January 29, 2009).

Tuggle, Justin L., and Malcolm D. Holmes. 2006. "Blowing Smoke: Status Politics and the Smoking Ban," pp. 151–61 in *Constructions of Deviance: Social Power, Context and Interaction*. 5th edn. Ed. P. A. Adler and P. Adler. Belmont, CA: Thompson Wadsworth.

Turner, Jill. 1999. "Dating for Money," pp. 32–6 in *Degrees of Deviance: Student Accounts of Their Deviant Behavior*. Ed. S. Henry and R. Eaton. Salem, WI: Sheffield Publishing Company.

Urban Dictionary. www.urbandictionary.com.

Victor, Jeffrey S. 1993. *Satanic Panic: The Creation of a Contemporary Legend*. Chicago: Open Court.

1998. "Moral Panics and the Social Construction of Deviant Behavior: Theory and Application to the Case of Ritual Child Abuse." *Sociological Perspectives*, 41: 541–65.

Vincent, Chuck. 1999. "Pressure to Drink," pp. 97–100 in *Degrees of Deviance: Student Accounts of Their Deviant Behavior*. Ed. S. Henry and R. Eaton. Salem, WI: Sheffield Publishing Company.

Weitz, Rose. 1993. "Living with the Stigma of AIDS," pp. 222–36 in *Deviant Behavior: A Test Reader in the Sociology of Deviance*. 4th edn. Ed. Dellos H. Kelly. New York: St. Martin's Press.

Wood, Staci Barker. 1999. "Stigma Management and Cystic Fibrosis," pp. 139–42 in *Degrees of Deviance: Student Accounts of Their Deviant Behavior*. Ed. S. Henry and R. Eaton. Salem, WI: Sheffield Publishing Company.

Index

abortion 5
Action on Smoking and Health
    (ASH) 30
Adler, Patricia A. 1
Adler, Peter 1
adultery
  judging deviance 5
  statistical analysis of 16–17
advocacy groups
  see interest groups
Aggelton, Peter 82, 85–6
AIDS Coalition to Unleash Power
    (ACT UP) 30
alcohol
  banning behavior 31–3
  as deviance 9
  motivations 67–8
  US Prohibition laws 33
Alcoholics Anonymous 9, 112
Altheide, David L. 117
Alvi, Shahid 125
American Self-Help
    Clearinghouse 112
Americans with Disabilities Act 119
animal rights activism
  judging deviance of 8–9

Animals Deserve Adequate Protection
    Today and Tomorrow (ADAPTT)
    9
appearance
  banning 27–8
  Muslim modesty 6–7
  positive deviance 107
  school shooters 49
  self and social identity 80–1
  see also obesity
attachment
  Bowlby's theory of 78
  conformity and 68–9

banning behavior
  appearances 27–8
  forcing problems underground 116
  ideas 26–7
  identifying differences 25–8
  law-making and 41–3
  moral entrepreneurs 30–5
  moral panics and 35–8
  social process of 30–8
Becker, Howard S.
  moral entrepreneurs 31
  Outsiders 23, 25–6

"Being Sane in Insane Places"
  (Rosenhan) 90–2
beliefs
  in conformity 68–9
  paranormal 26
Believe the Children 37
Ben-Yehuda, Norman
  Moral Panics (with Goode) 35, 36
Bender, Eugene I. 111
Berger, Peter 124
biological factors
  motivations and 14–16
Bogdan, Robert 120
Bowlby, John
  attachment theory 78, 81
Box, Steven 80
Bradley, Bud 68
Brekhus, Wayne
  "Mundane Manifesto" 54–5
  "A Sociology of the Unmarked"
  55
Brown, A. 80–1
Brown, Patricia Lee 111
bullying 47–8
  school shooters and 50

Cast Off Your Old Tired Ethics
  (COYOTE) 30
Center for Disease Control
  on school shooters 50
children
  forming identities 76–8, 83–4
  parenting and 7–8
  satanic abuse and 35–8
  sexual abuse of 53
Citizens Against Child Abuse 37
civil disobedience 9
civil rights movement 116
Clark, Winston 60, 62, 63
CLOUT 37
Cohen, Stanley
  Folk Devils and Moral Panics 35
communications technology
  mass media and 41
conformity
  formation of social self 79–80
  general commitment to 57

reasons for 46
  without commitment to 68–72
Cooley, Charles Horton 78
Copes, Heath
  "Excuses, Excuses" (with
  Maruna) 65
Craft, Elizabeth A. 100–2, 117
Cressey, Donald
  on vocabulary 58–9
crime
  mass media and 40–1, 124–5
  self-control and 71
  television culture and 38
Crocker, Jennifer 95, 96
  positive deviance 106–8
cultural conflicts
  changing climate of 21
  competing demands of 6–7
  constructing deviance 6–8
  universal values 13

De Young, Mary
  on satanic abuse 36–7
DeKesredy, Walter S. 125
deviance
  acceptability range 44–7
  biographical contexts of 47–8
  extreme and mundane 53–6
  identity status 81–4
  institutional 54
  labels and 24
  measuring 16–20
  mutual aid 110–16
  normality and difference 2–4
  politics of 122–3
  positive 3, 16, 17, 106–8
  range of 57
  recognizing difference 123–4
  redefining 109–10, 116–20
  social construction of 4–9
  society's uncertainties 1
  see also motivation
Deviant Behavior (journal) 23
difference
  normality and 2–4
  political correctness 21–2
  recognizing 123–4

disabilities
  banned appearances 27
  social judgment 81–2
The Disreputable Pleasures (Hagan)
  18–20
Dovidio, John F. 96
  positive deviance 106–8
drugs
  NORML 30, 113, 119
  peer pressure 84
Durkheim, Emile
  common consciousness 17

Eakin, Emily 55
Eaton, Roger 62
  motives for deviation 66
Elite Deviance (Simon) 54
Ellis, Desmond 125
endorphins 15
enjoyment of deviance 66
Everyone's Doing It! (Gabor) 63
"Excuses, Excuses" (Maruna and
  Copes) 65
experts
  satanic menace 36–8

Fairchild, Carol 60, 61
families
  parenting 7–8
Federal Bureau of Investigation
  Lessons Learned on school
    shootings 50
Folk Devils and Moral Panics
  (Cohen) 35
Frost, Janet 64
Furlong, Michael J. 50

Gabor, Thomas
  Everyone's Doing It! 63
Garfinkel, Harold 90
genetic factors
  motivations and 14
Goffman, Erving 90, 124
  discreditable and discredited
    96
  diversion and deflection 98
  front and back stages 89

social selves 80
spoiled identity 95
Good, Tyrone 63, 66
Goode, Erich 53, 128
  audience's perception 18
  difference and deviance 3–4
  judgments of deviance 5
  Moral Panics (with Ben-Yehuda)
    35, 36
  politics of deviance 122–3
  qualities of negative deviance 17
  sociological perspectives 1
  study of deviance 22–3
Gottfredson, Michael R. 70–2
gun ownership 52
Gusfield, Joseph 33

Hagan, John
  The Disreputable Pleasures 18–20
Hanson, F. Allan 82
harm
  denial of 60
  seriousness of 20
  victims of 60–2
  see also pain and suffering
Harris, Eric 52
Hawkins, Robert 75–6
health and safety
  creating deviance 10
  power structures and 19–20
Heckert, Alex 85
  positive deviance 106, 107
Heckert, Druann Maria 85
  positive deviance 106, 107
Heimer, Karen 88
Heitzig, Nancy A. 27, 105
  social reordering 115–16
Hendershott, Anne 123
  The Politics of Deviance 21, 22,
    23
Henry, Stuart
  on banning 25
  concealing stigma 100
  deviant groups 110
  on mass media 39
  motives for deviation 66
  mutual aid groups 113–14

Henry (cont.)
   positive deviance 107
   self-denial 105
   self-labeling 87
   theory of office 89
Hirschi, Travis
   failure to conform 68–72
HIV/AIDS
   deviant identity and 82–3
   secrecy and 99–100
   stigmatization 85–6
Holmes, Malcolm D. 34
honesty, statistical deviance of 57
"honor" killlings 6–7

ideas, challenging 26–7
identity
   avoidance and dropping out 104–5
   building normality 120–1
   coping with stigma 102–5
   as deviant 75–8, 81–4
   dominant groups and stigma 85–6
   formation of 78–9
   from institutional handling 89–92
   labeling 24, 85–8
   managing secrecy 97–102
   "music tribes" 83–4
   mutual aid groups 110–16
   others' reaction to stigma 108
   personal biographies and 73
   Robert Hawkin's case 75–6
   self-labeling 87
   the social self 79–81
illness
   alcoholism as 9
   coping by secrecy 93–101
   stigma 108
individuals
   behind the label 118
   biographies and contexts of 11,
      47–8, 72–4
   isolation of 113
   justification by ledger 62–3
institutions
   classifying deviants 89–92
intentions
   denial of negative intent 63–4

interest groups
   banning behavior 30
   mutual aid 111–16
   postmodern view 21
   use of media 38–41
Internet
   expressing deviancy 117–18
   mass media and 41

Japan
   elevator behavior 55
   Journal of Mundane Behavior 54, 55

Katz, Alfred H. 111
King, Susan 27–8
Kinkle, Kip 51
kinship groups
   adultery and 5–6
Klebold, Dylan 52
Klockars, Carl
   Professional Fence 63

labeling and stigma
   coping with 93–7
   as deviant 85–6
   discreditable and discredited 96–7
   institutional 89–92
   mutual aid groups 110–16
   overcoming 102–3
   positive deviance 106–8
   self-labeling 88
   theory of office 88–92
   see also identity; stereotypes
Lanier, Mark 69
Larkin, Philip 52
laws and rules
   banning behavior 30, 41–3
   consensus on crime 18–19
   copyright and piracy 17–18
   making of 24
   moral authority of 17
   mundane rule-breaking 55–6
   neutralizing bind of 59
   power structures of 19–20
   promote values 10
   seriousness of harm 20
   see also public policy

Lee, James Daniel 100–2, 117
Lee, Yeuh-Ting 85
Lemert, Edwin 77
Levine, Murray 115
Liazos, Alexander
  institutional deviance 54
Lockhart, Lisa 61
Louganis, Greg 99
loyalties, justification by 62

Major, Brenda 95, 96, 102
  positive deviance 106–8
Malone, Scott 61
Martin, Daniel D. 115
Maruna, Shadd
  "Excuses, Excuses" (with Copes)
    65
mass media
  agenda building 40
  crime stories 124–5
  interaction with society
    38–9
  learning deviance by 117
  public perceptions 19
Matsueda, Ross 77, 79
  labeling 87
Matza, David 56
  neutralizing bind of law 59
Mead, George Herbert 78–9
media
  see mass media
Media, Crime and Criminal Justice
  (Surette) 39
mental illness
  pseudo-patients study 90–2
Michaels, Jay 64
Miller, Carol T. 95
  coping with stigma 102–5
Miller, L. 88
Mills, Martin 98–9
Mississippi
  restaurants and BMI 41–2
money and material gain
  as motive for deviance 66
moral entrepreneurs 30–5
  disabilities groups 119–20
  satanic panic and 36–8

moral panic 10
  creation of 35–8
Moral Panics: The Social
    Construction of Deviance
    (Goode and Ben-Yehuda) 35, 36
morality
  common consciousness 17
  condemning condemners 62
  inhibitions 24
  neutralizing 59–65
  pain and suffering and 12–13
  relativism 12, 21
Moss, Louis 64
Mothers Against Drunk Driving
    (MADD) 31
motivation 24
  biological/genetic factors 14–16
  engaging in deviance 13–16
  failure to conform 68–72
  human biographies and contexts
    72–4
  justification vocabulary 58–9, 65
  neutralization theory and 57–65
  rational-choice thinkers 71–2
  rewards for deviance 65–8
"Mundane Manifesto" (Brekhus)
    54–5
Muslim cultures
  modest dress and 6–8
mutual aid groups 110–16
  help against stigma 112–13
  personal accounts and 117

National Association to Advance Fat
    Acceptance (NAAFA) 115
National Organization for the
    Reform of Marijuana Laws
    (NORML) 30, 111, 119
Nesbeth, M. 55
neutralization theory 56
  appeal to higher authorities 62
  condemning condemners 62
  injury denial 60
  metaphor of the ledger 62–3, 103
  negative intent denial 63–4
  normality claim 63
  privilege to deviate claim 64–5

neutralization theory (cont.)
  relative acceptability claim 64
  responsibility denial 60
  victim denial 60–2
  vocabulary of motives 57–9, 65
Newman, Katherine
  Rampage 49–52
normal
  becoming 120–1
  difference and normality 2–4
  see also conformity
norms
  different groups 4–5
  justification by claiming 63
  laws and 10
  many realities and 10
North, Tom 64

obesity
  as deviance 9
  Mississippi restaurant law 41–2
  motivation and 14
  mutual aid groups 115
  sense of self and 82
Odd Man In (Sagarin) 105
office, theory of 12, 88–92
Outsiders: Studies in the Sociology of Deviance (Becker) 23, 25–6
Overeaters Anonymous 115

Page, Andy 67–8
pain and suffering
  pleasure in 53–4
  relative morality and 12–13
  sharing 113–14
Papua New Guinea
  views of adultery 5–6
parents
  of school shooters 50
  secure emotional base 78
Park, Kristin 98, 105
Parker, Richard 82, 85–6
Parvez, Aqsa 6–7, 21
  motivation 14
Parvez, Muhammad 6–7
peer pressure
  metaphor of the ledger 103

People for the Ethical Treatment of Animals (PETA) 9
Pershing, Jana 62
Pfuhl, Erwin H.
  on banning 25
  concealing stigma 100
  deviant groups 110
  on mass media 39
  mutual aid groups 113–14
  self-labeling 87
  theory of office 89
piracy and copyright law 17–18
political contexts 122–3
  changing 21
  as motive for deviance 66–7
The Politics of Deviance (Hendershott) 21, 22, 23
popular culture
  school shooters and 51
postmodernism
  decentralized groups and 21
power structures
  banning and 28–9
  institutional deviance 54
  labeling and 85
  law-making process 19–20
  see also public policy
problem-solving
  as motive for deviance 66
Professional Fence (Klockars) 63
public opinion
  media and 39–41
public policy
  criminal justice 40–1
  difference and 21–2

Quinn, Harley 26–7

racism, challenging 26–7
Rampage: The Social Roots of School Shootings (Newman) 49–52
relativism 1
religion
  justification by 62
Resource Center for Independent Living 118
responsibility, denial of 60

restaurants
  tipping and stiffing 11–12, 88
Rhee, Sujin Sabrina 50
Riessman, Frank 112
Robinson, David
  mutual aid groups 114–15
positive deviance 107
self-denial 105
Rosenhan, D. L.
  "Being Sane in Insane Places" 90–2
Sagarin, Edward 110
  mutual aid groups 115
San Diego Country Policy Panel on
  Odd Man In 105
Youth and Alcohol 31–3
San Diego Police Officers' Association 31–3
San Diego State University
  study of deviance 22–3
Satanic Panic (Victor) 37–8
  satanism and cult worship 10, 26
  moral panic over 35–8
  school shooters and 51–2
The Scapegoat Society 104
scapegoating 104
Schaffer, Scott 55
schools
  boys' violence and 98–9
  peer abuse 50–1
  rampage shootings 48–53, 61–2, 66
  social pressures 47–8
Schur, Edwin
  stigma contests 120
secrecy
  managing stigma 97–102
self-control
  failure to conform 69–72
  as social control 79
self-fulfilling outcomes 88
self-help groups
  see mutual aid groups
sex and sexuality
  cyber-porn surfers 66
  extreme deviance 53
  homosexuality 46–7
  judging deviance 5–6

politics of 66–7
  relative acceptability claim 64–5
  secrecy and 99–100
statistical analysis of behavior 16–17
universal incest taboo
sex workers
  control and 67
  lap dancing 44–7
  sexually transmitted diseases 117
    see also HIV/AIDS
Sharma, Bonita 50
Shaw, Karen 67
Shea, Jennifer 64, 65
Simon, David
  Elite Deviance 54
Smart, Laura 99, 100
SmokeFree Illinois 8
smoking
  changing context of 8
  consensus on 19
  moral entrepreneurs 34
  social audiences
  deviance construction 25
  hierarchies of 28–9
  as motive for deviance 66
  no attachment to 68
  perception of deviance 18
  public discussion of behavior 19
  shaming and ostracism 19–20
  who judges deviance 5
social change
  mutual aid groups 115–16
  social constructionism 122
  constructing deviance 4–9
  norms and values of groups 4–5
  process of 10–13, 23–4
  sociological controversies 1–2
Social Issues Research Centre 83–4
social relationships
  disruption of 5–6
social theory
  critical 26–7
society
  celebration of order 17
  contexts constructing deviance 6
  interest in deviance 124–5
  politics of deviance 122

society (cont.)
uncertainties 1
see also social audiences
sociology
sensation-seeking theory 15–16
sociobiology
controversies within 1–2
studying deviance 20–3
The Sociology of Deviance: An
Obituary (Summer) 20, 22–3
"A Sociology of the Unmarked"
(Brekhus) 55
Sonenshein, Scott 106
Spritzer, Gretchen 106
Stafford, Gina 60
statistics of deviance 16
Steele, C. 95
stereotypes
construction of 11
control by 10
general use of 84–5
power structures 85–6
school social hierarchies 28–9
self-fulfilling prophecies 11–12
social judgement 81–2
tippers and stiffers 88
stigma
see labelling and stigma
Sudnow, David 89
Sullum, Jacob 28
Sumner, Colin
The Sociology of Deviance 20, 22–3
Surette, Ray 35–6
Media, Crime and Criminal Justice 39
public policy 39
Swaggi, Vincent 63

Tate, Katherine 3
Taylor, S. 120
terrorism
or activism? 9
paramilitary culture 52
Tuggle, Justin L. 34
Turner, Jill 63, 67
Vail, D. Angus 53
values
different groups and 4–5
"universal" 10
vegetarianism 116, 118
victims
creating deviance 10
denial of 60–2
Victor, Jeffrey
Satanic Panic 37–8
violence
boys' peer pressure 98–9
rampage shootings 48–53, 66
Wegner, Daniel M. 99, 100
Weight Watchers 9, 115
Weitz, Rose 100, 101
witches
Salem trials 3–4
Women's Christian Temperance
Movement 33
Wood, Staci Barker 93–5, 97, 101, 102
Woodham, Luke 61–2
Yourofsky, Gary 8–9, 14
Yueh-Ting Lee 85
Zine, Jasmine 6–7